Adult Coloring

by Two Hoots Coloring

NIMAL KINGDOM

animals out the wazoo.

Tips For Using This Book

1. We have printed the pictures on one side of the page only for the protection of each individual picture. A sheet of loose paper under the page you are working on will offer additional protection to the pages underneath.

2. Start with any page that grabs your interest - who says you need to start at the beginning?

3. Be free and color how YOU desire. There is no "wrong" way.

4. For a stress-relieving coloring experience, reduce noise and other distractions while coloring. Coloring with focus and intention is calming and nourishing for your spirit.

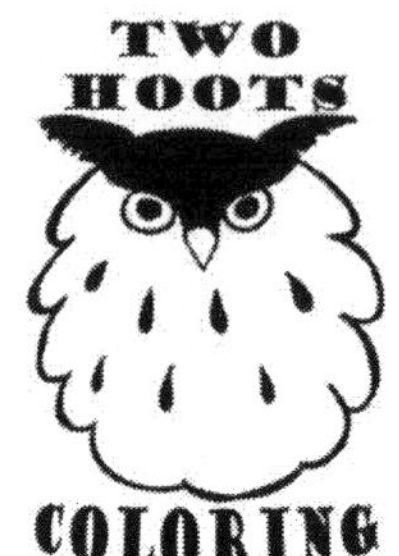

Adult Coloring Book: Animal Kingdom
By: Two Hoots Coloring

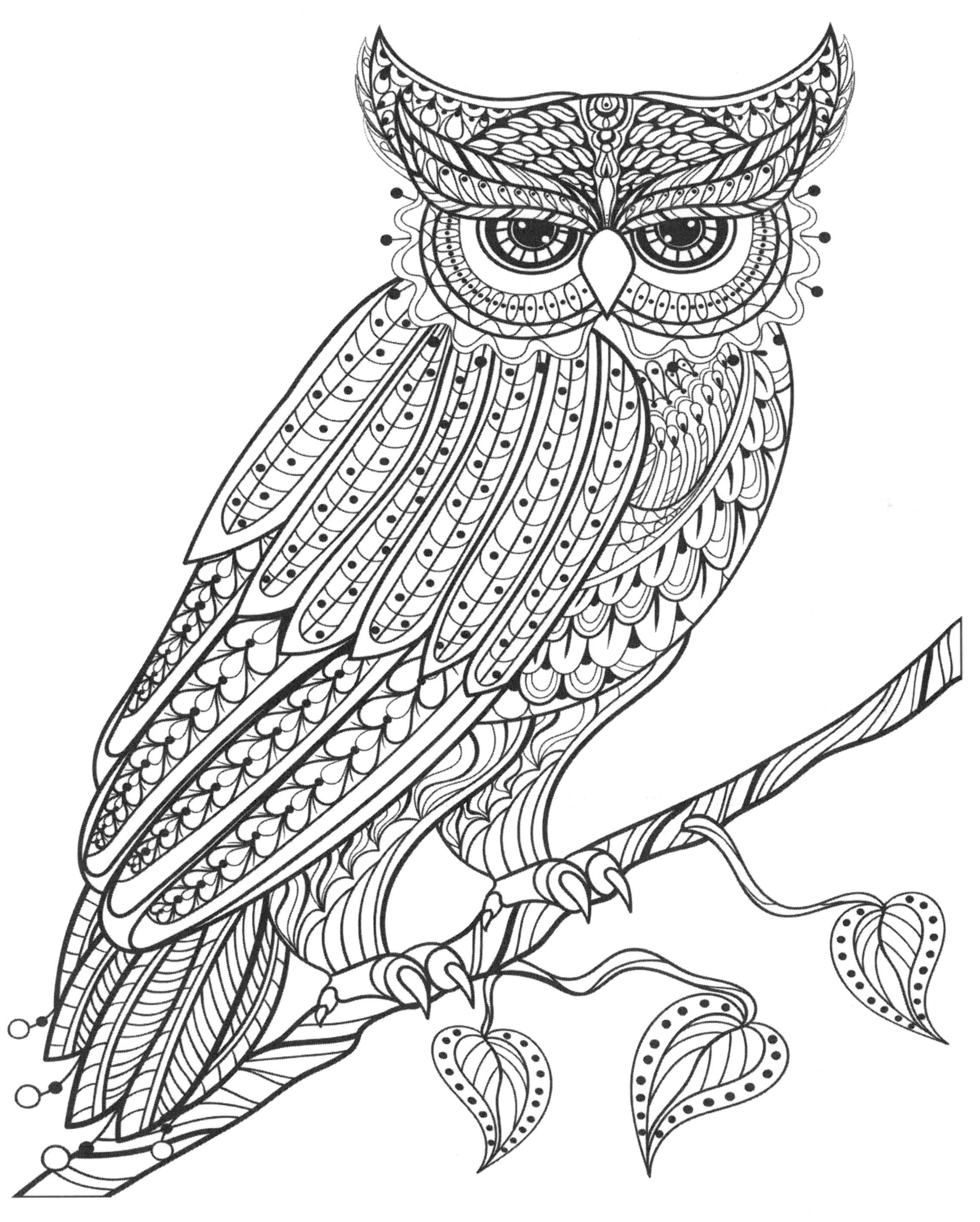

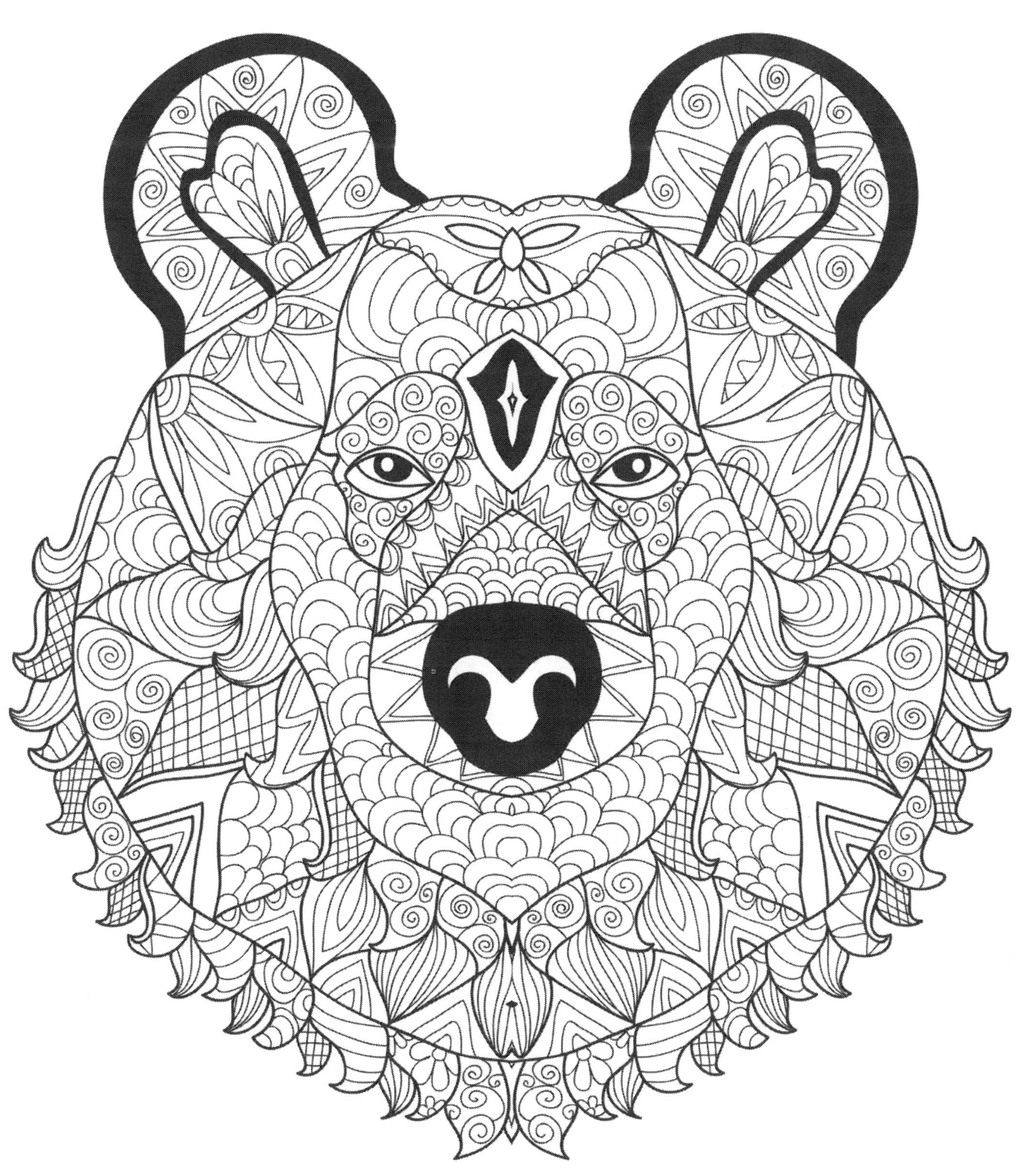

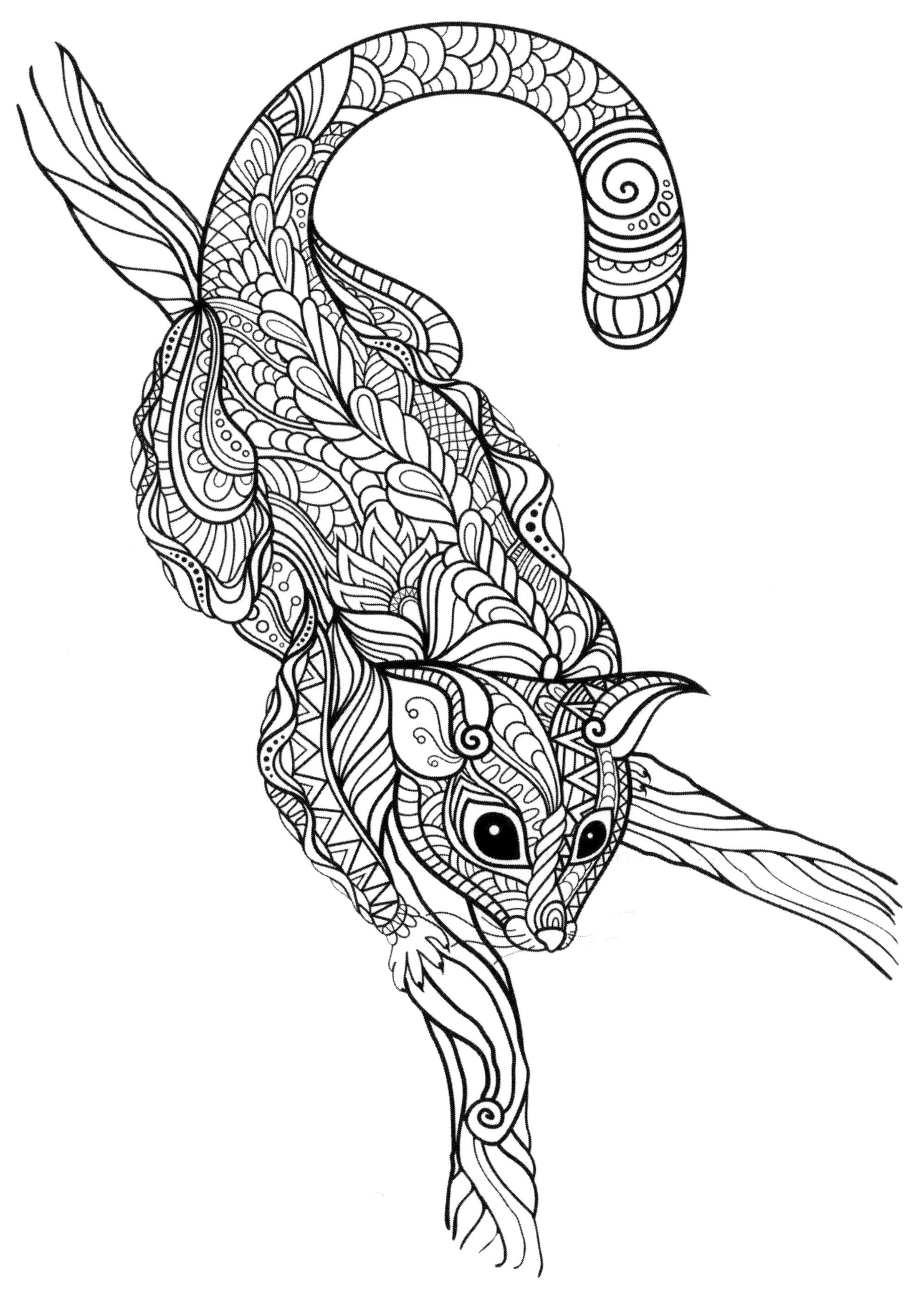

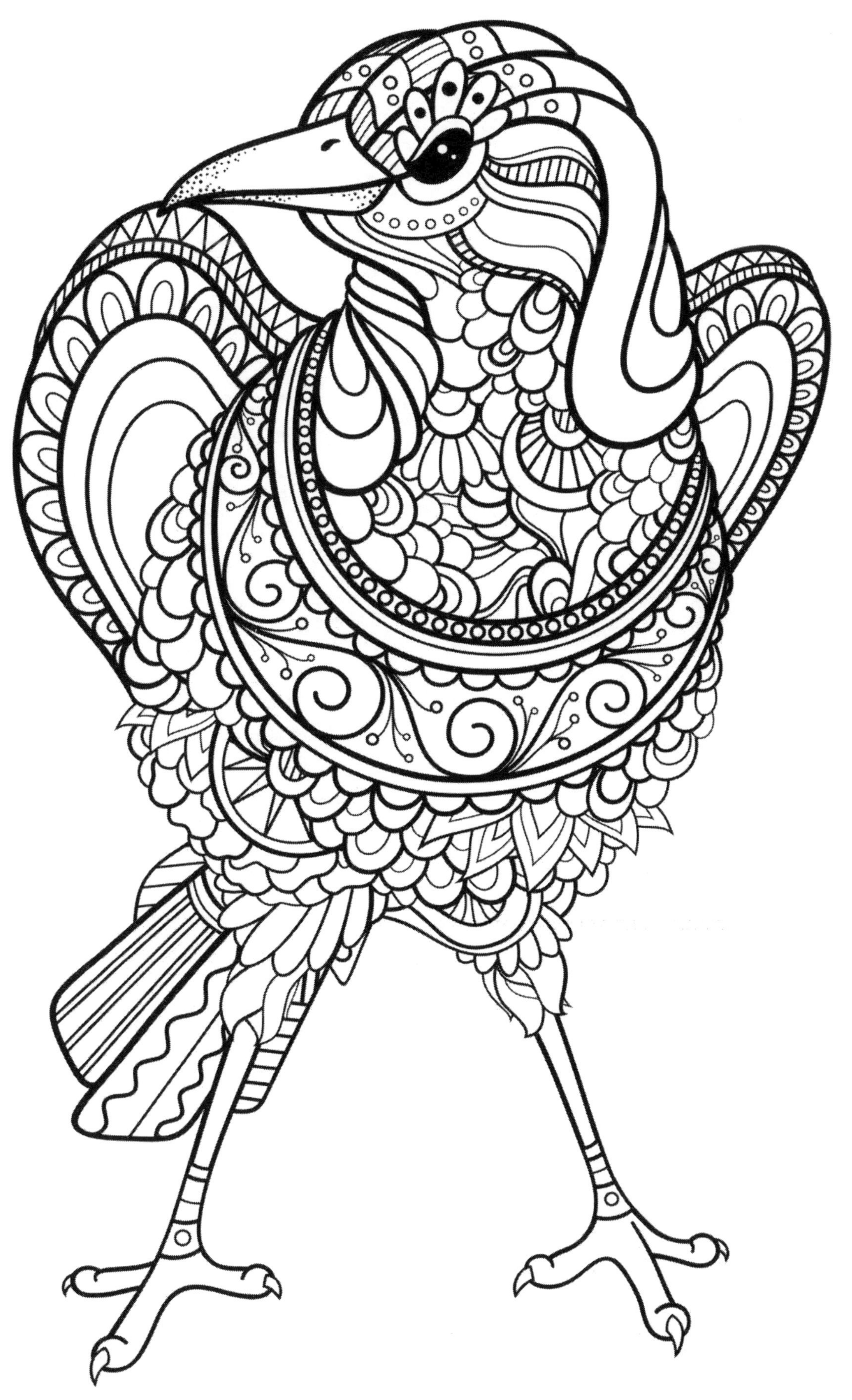

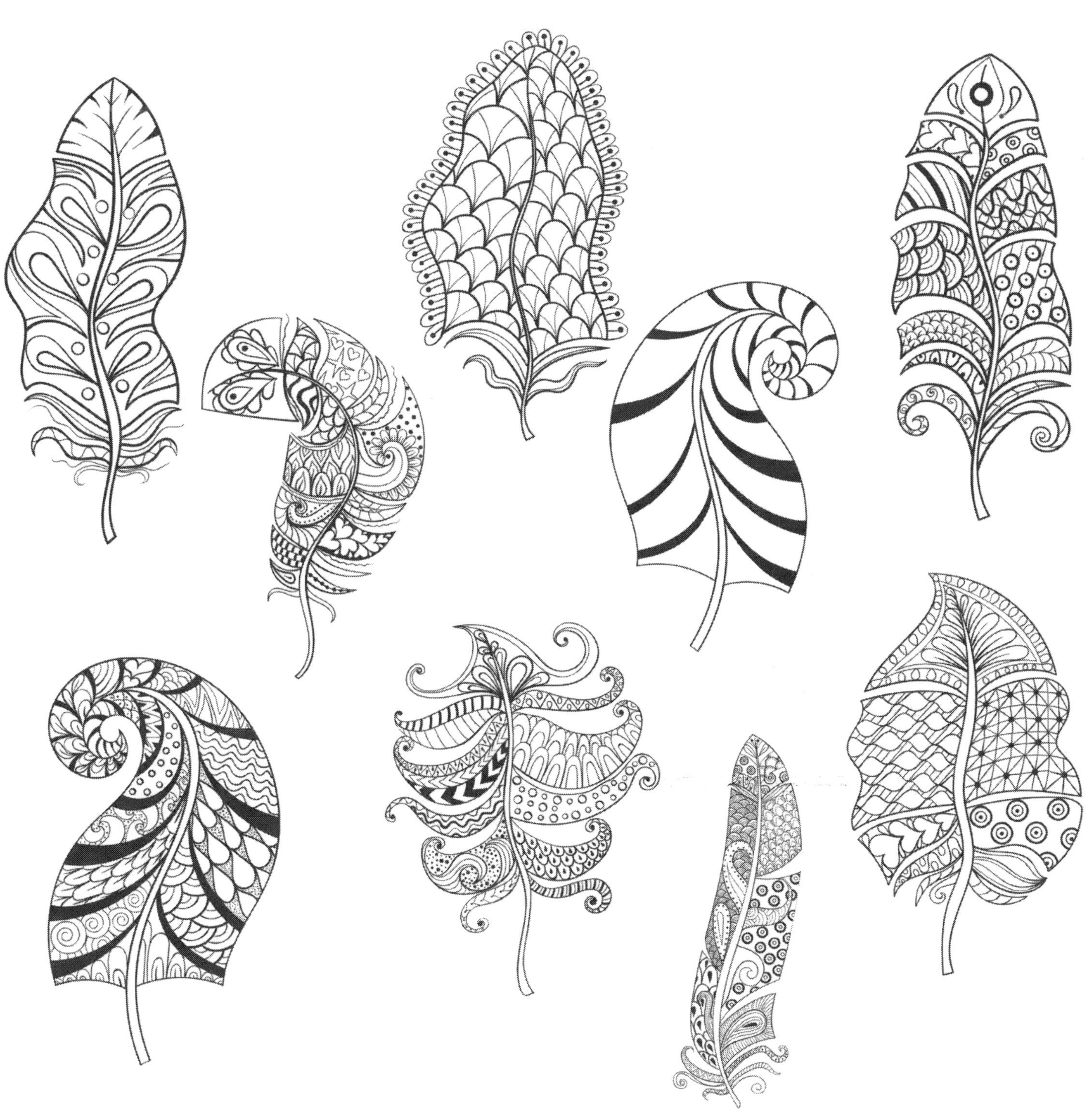

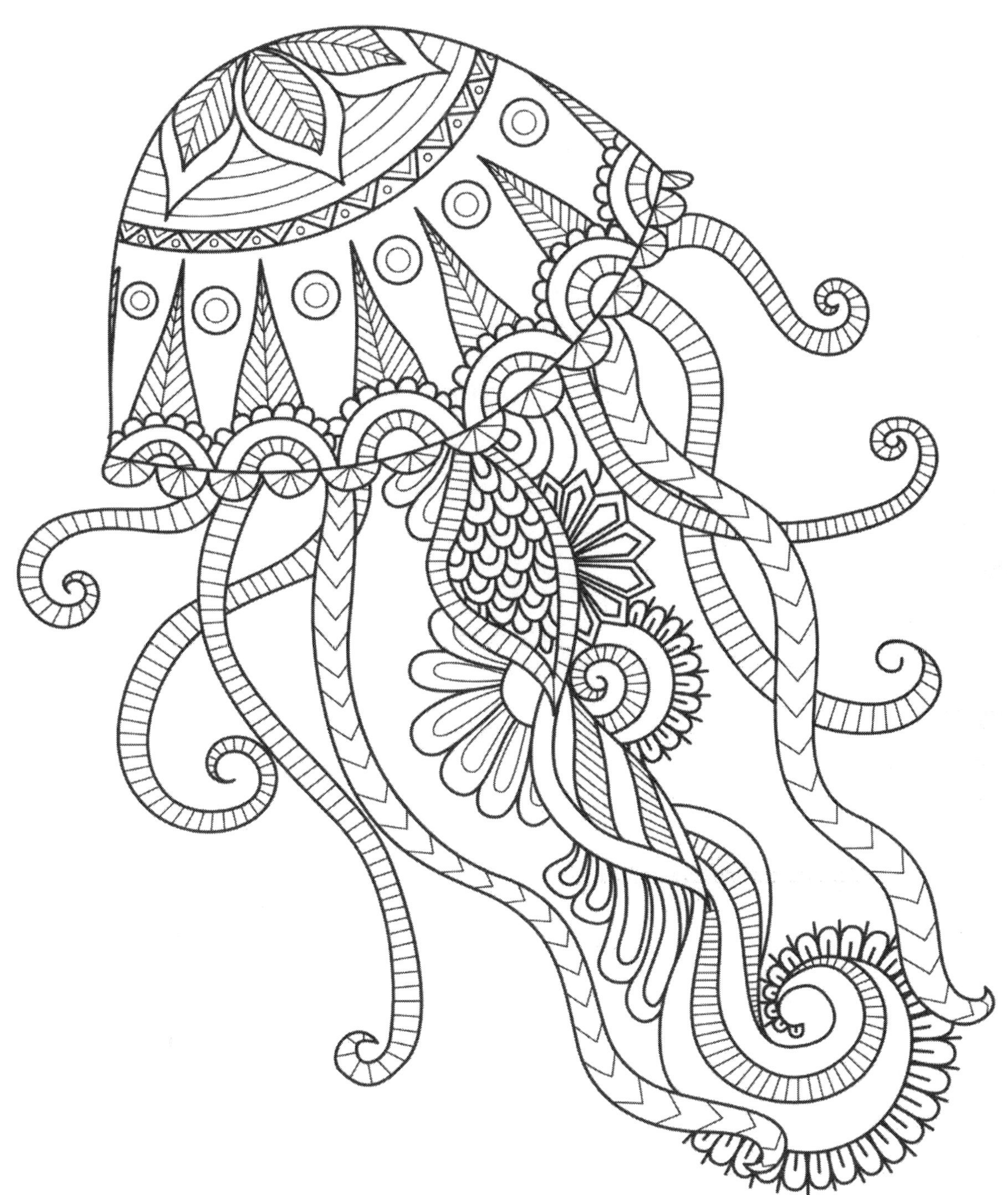

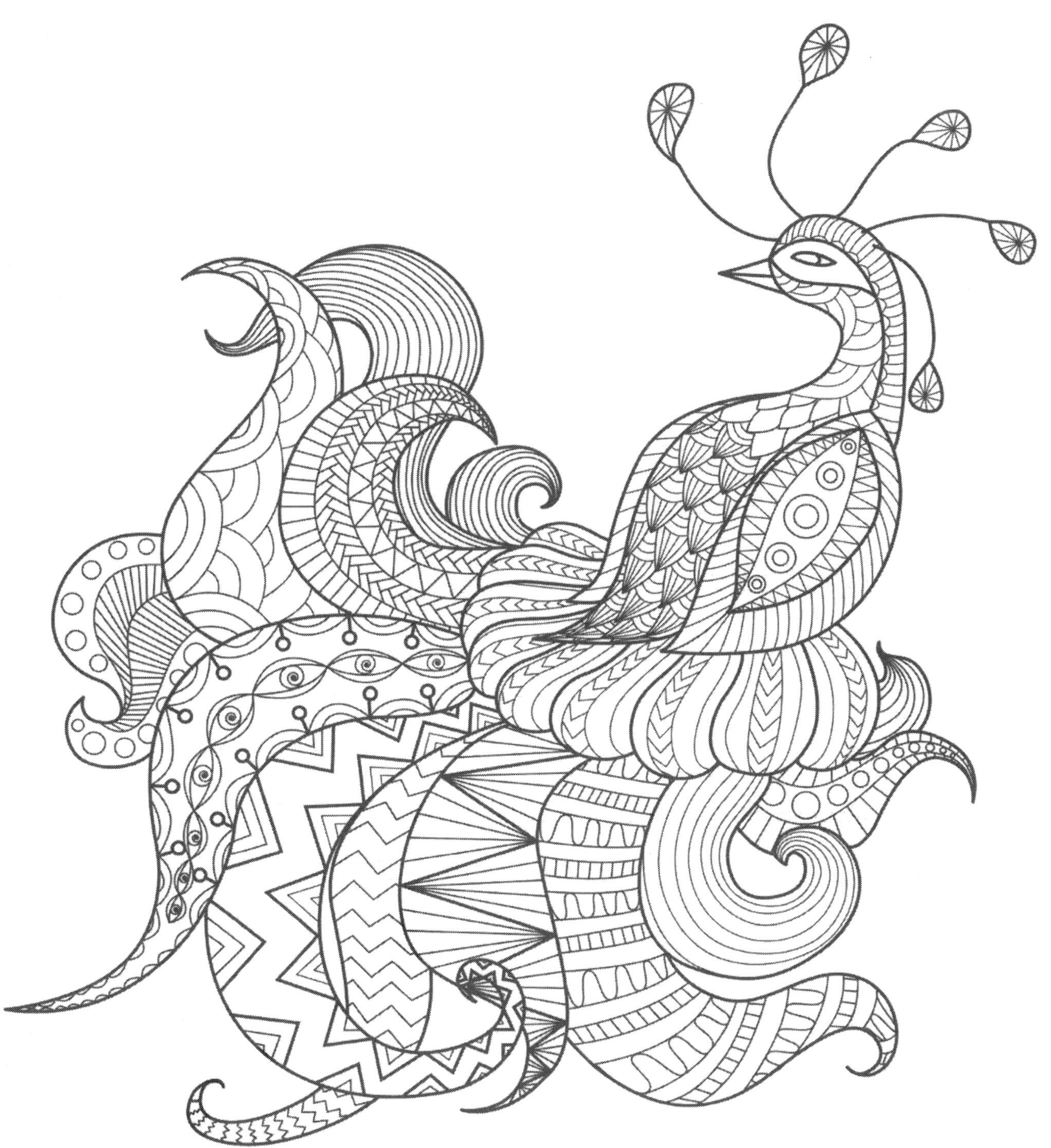

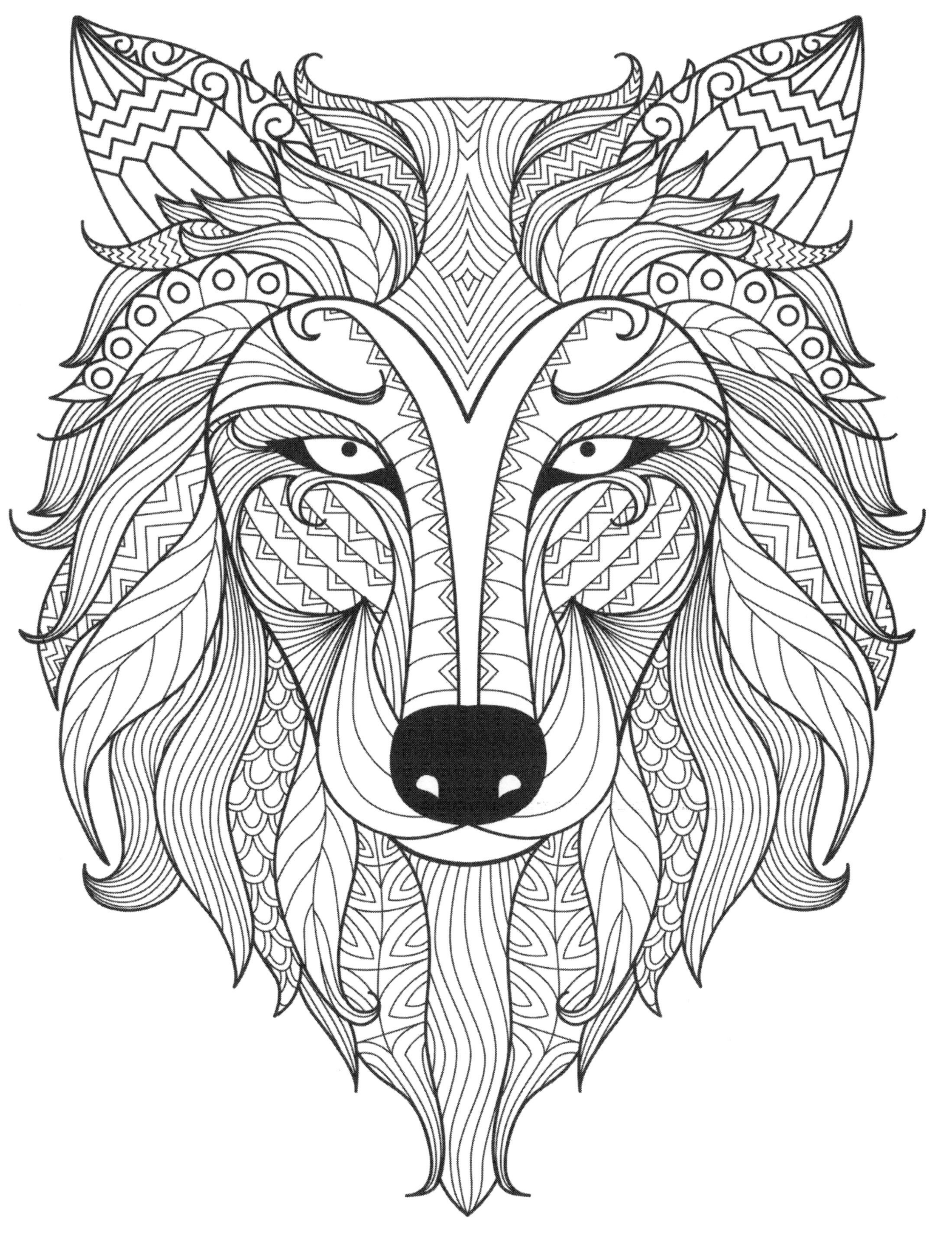

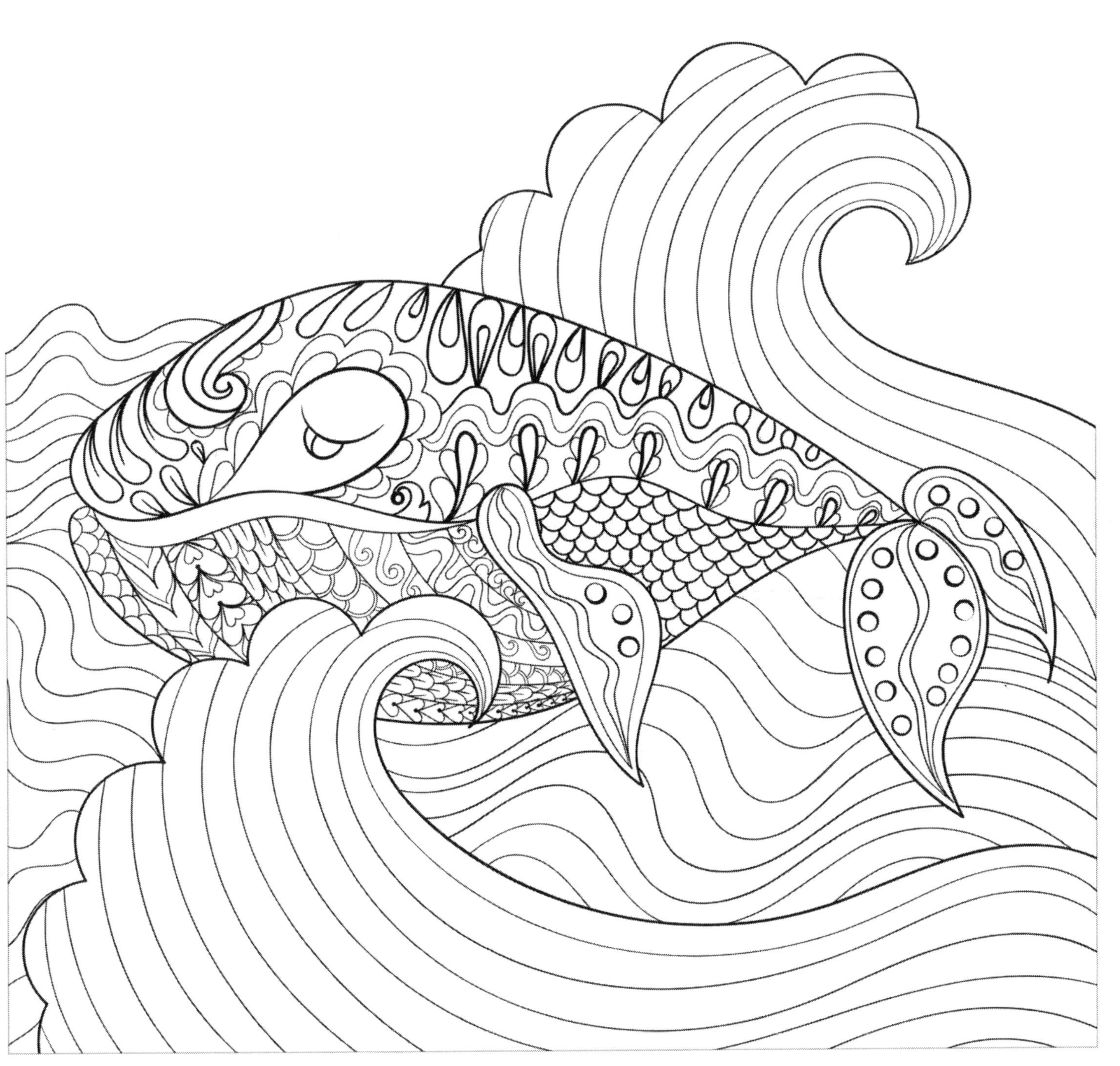

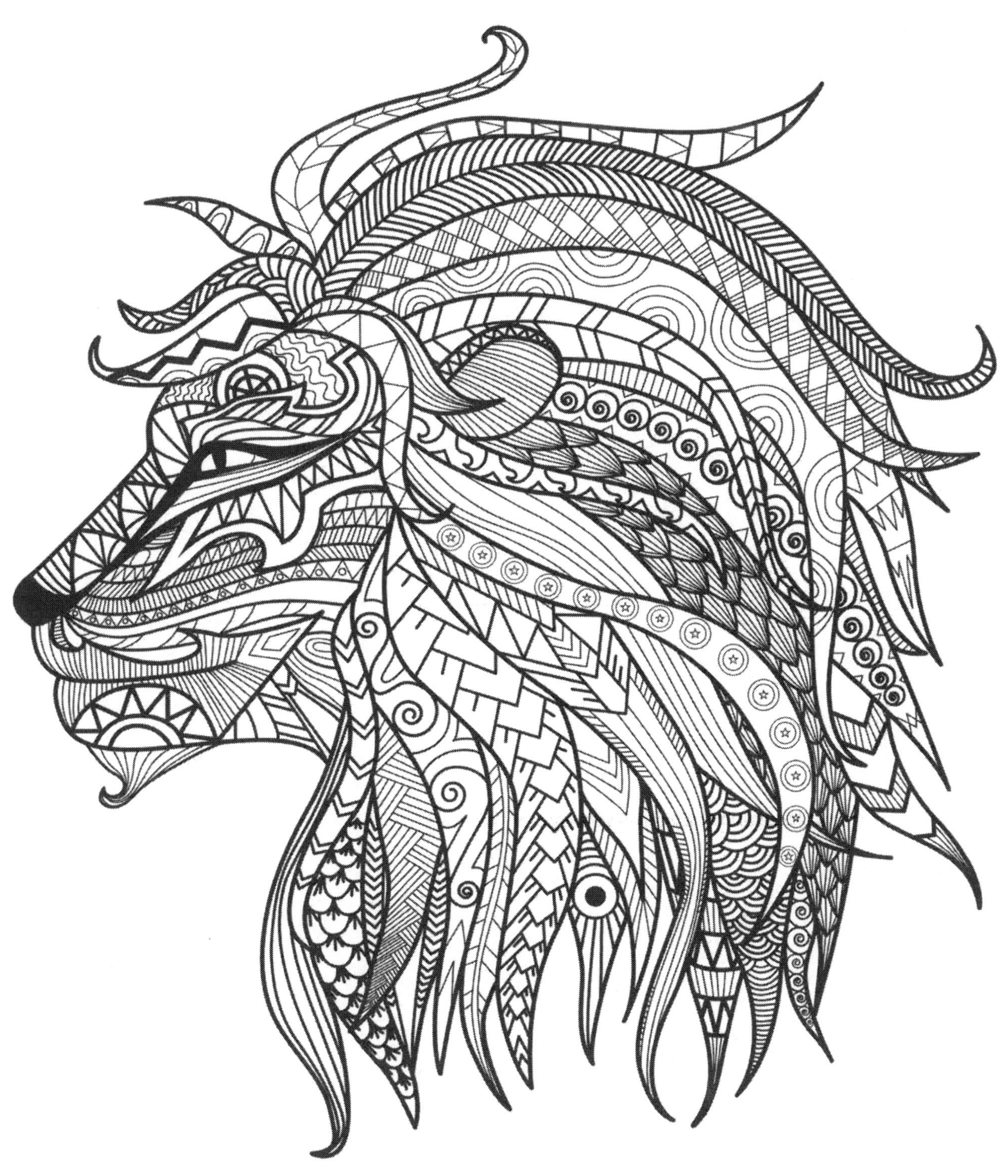

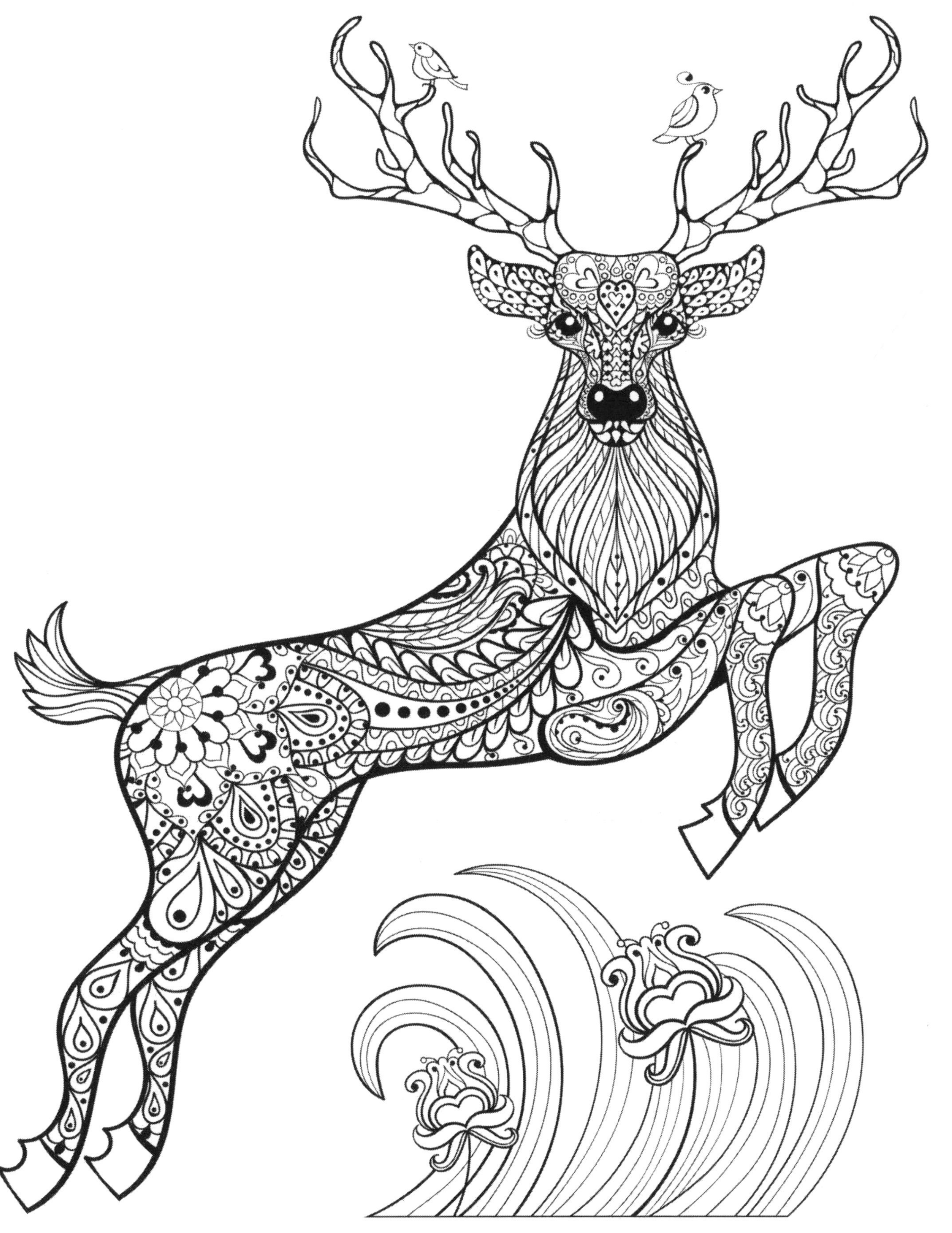

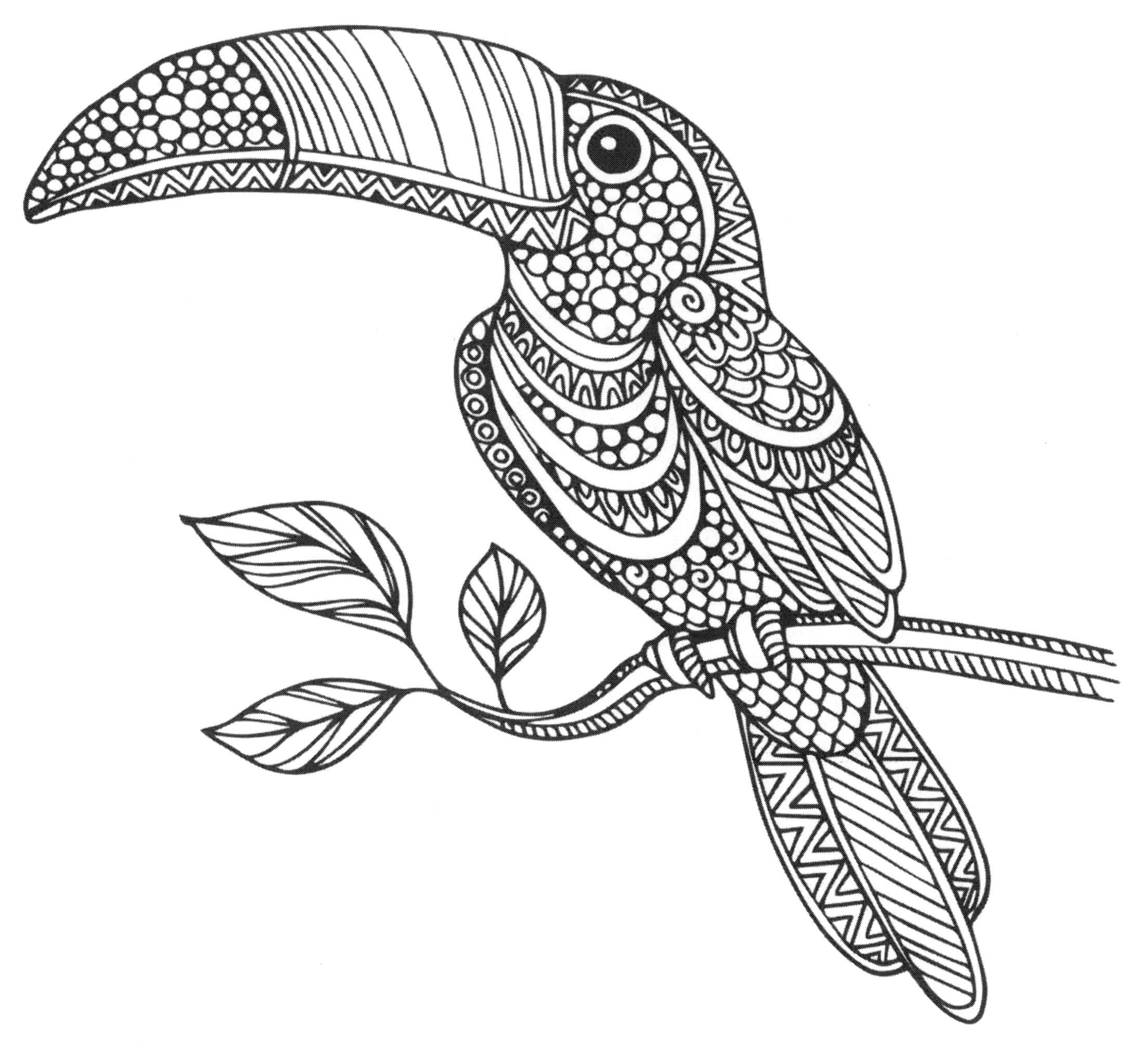

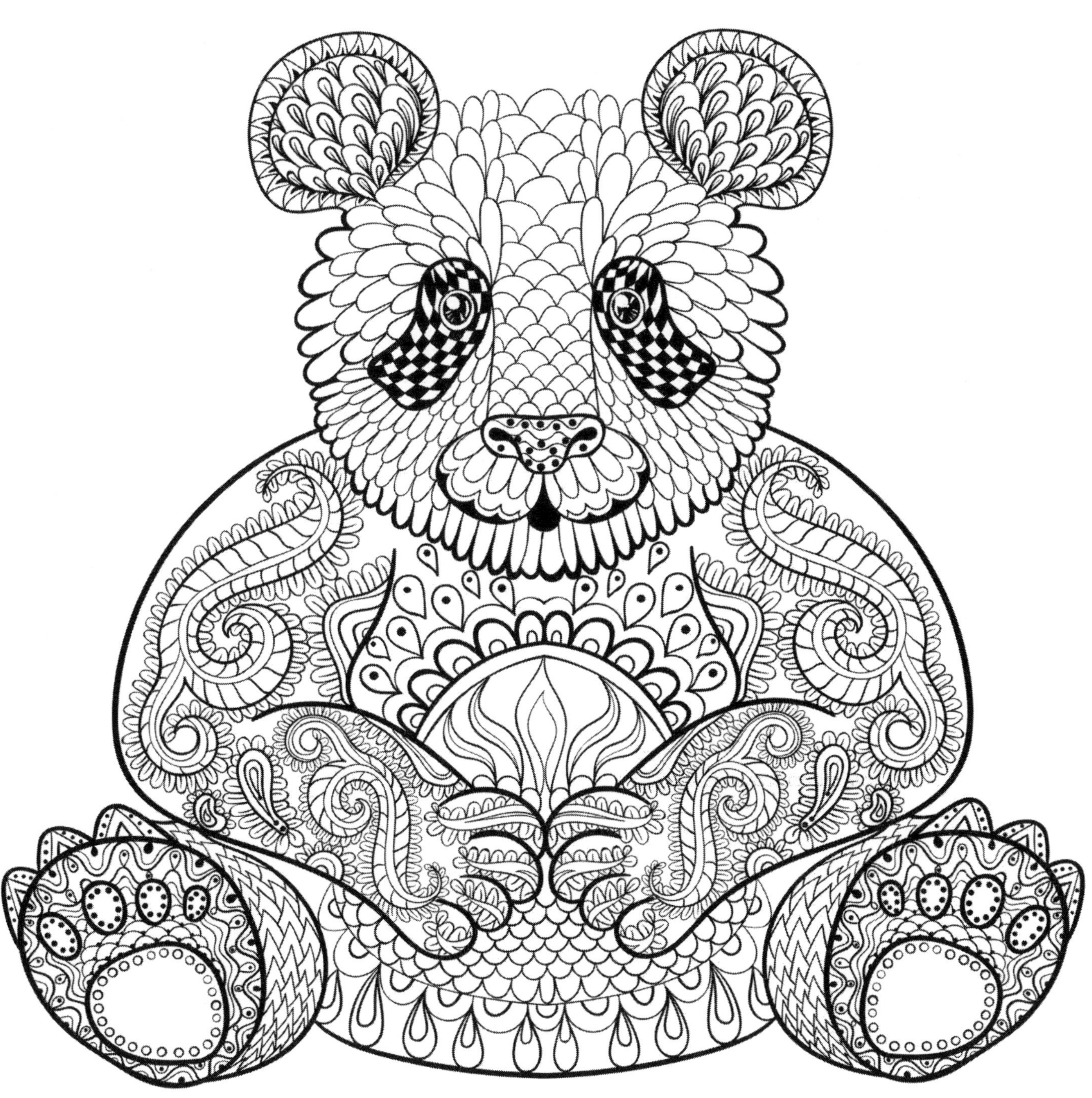

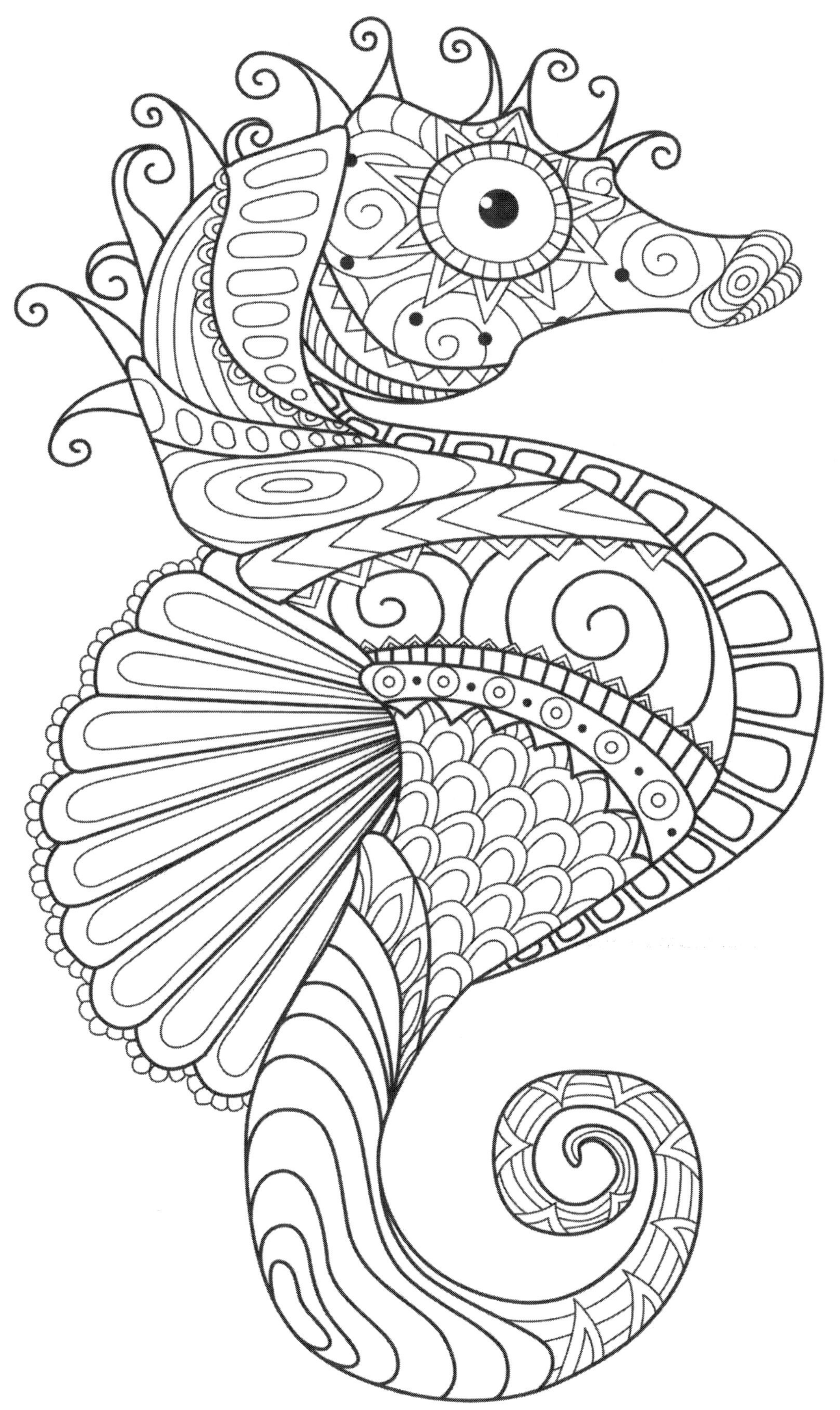

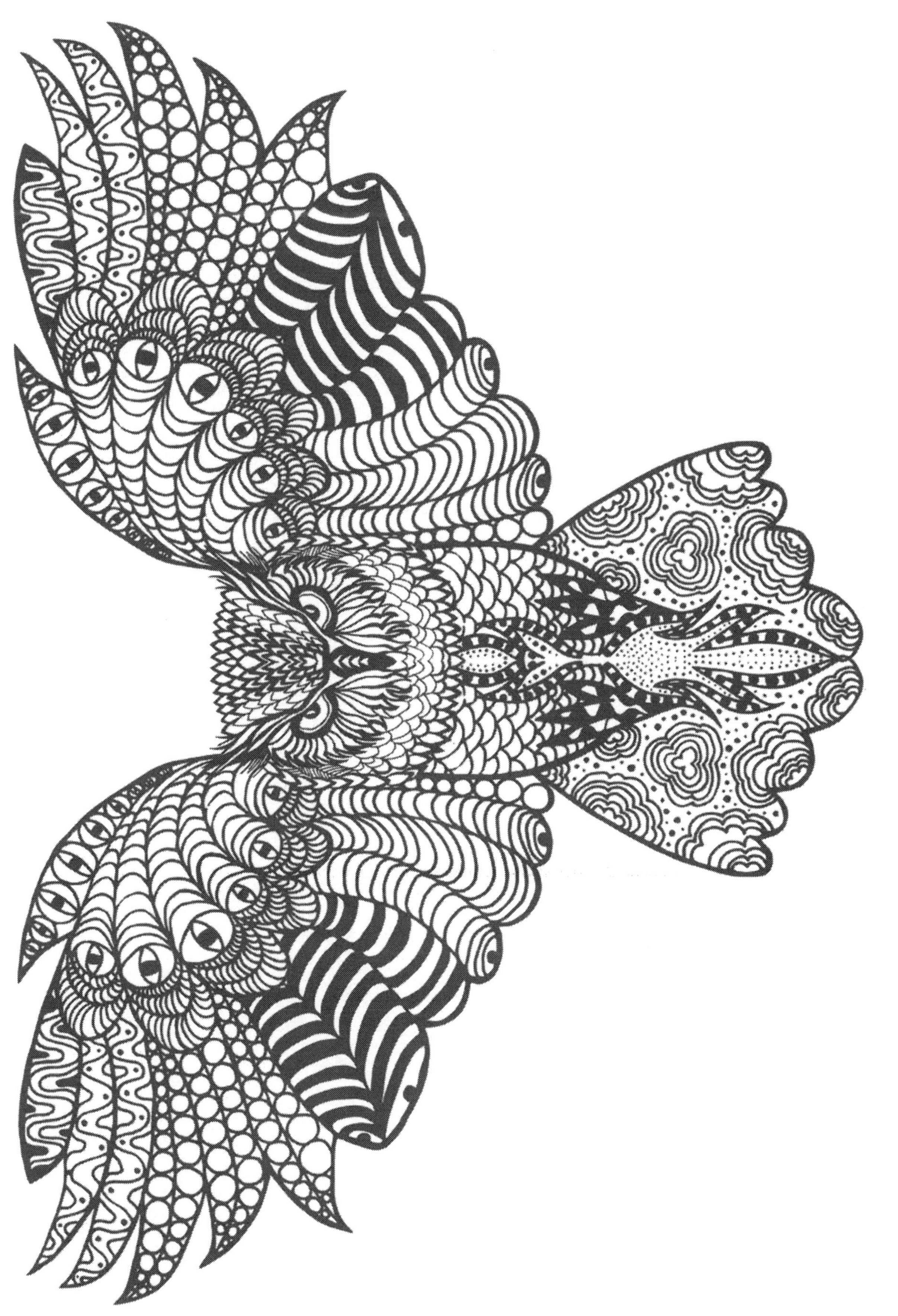

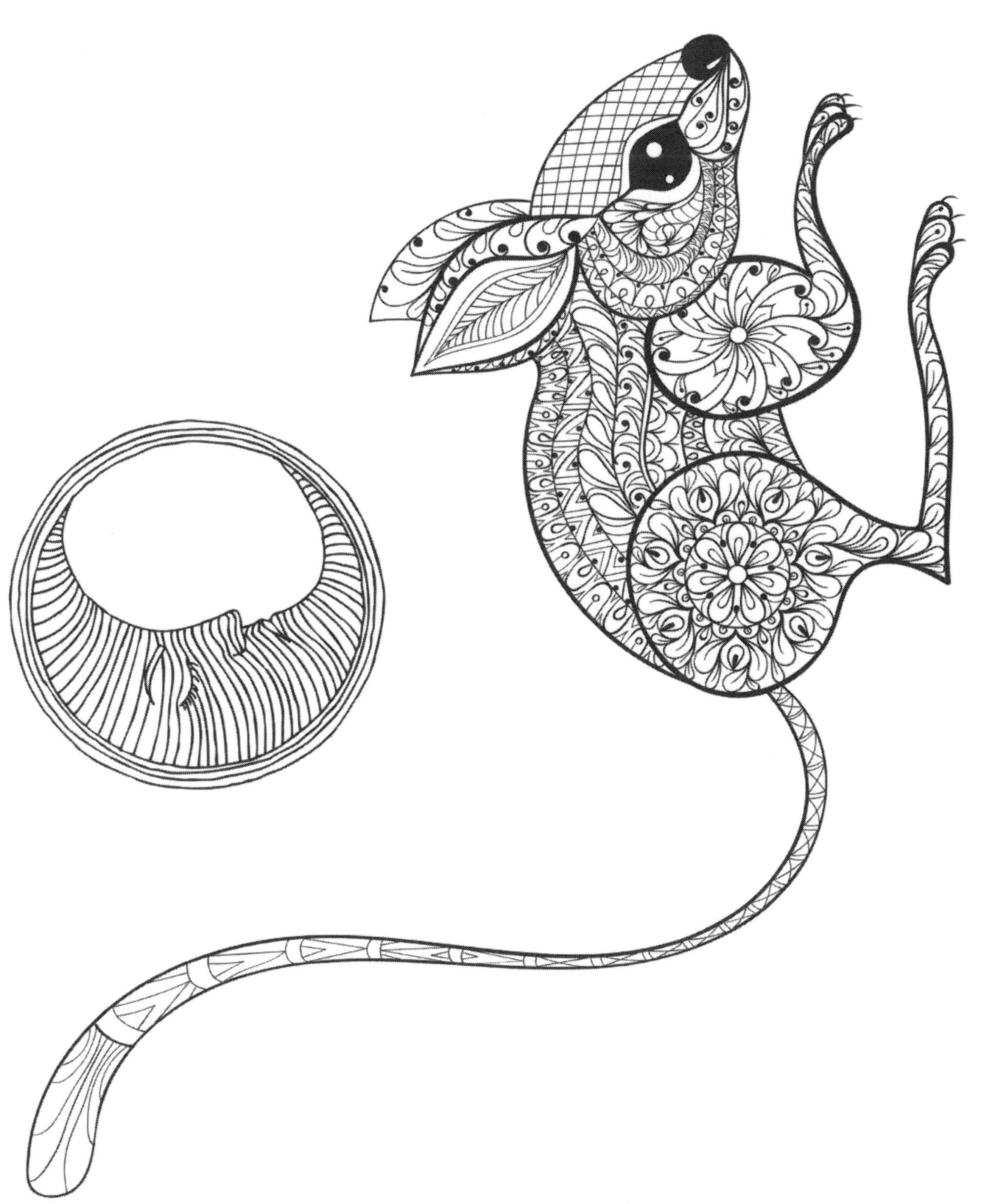

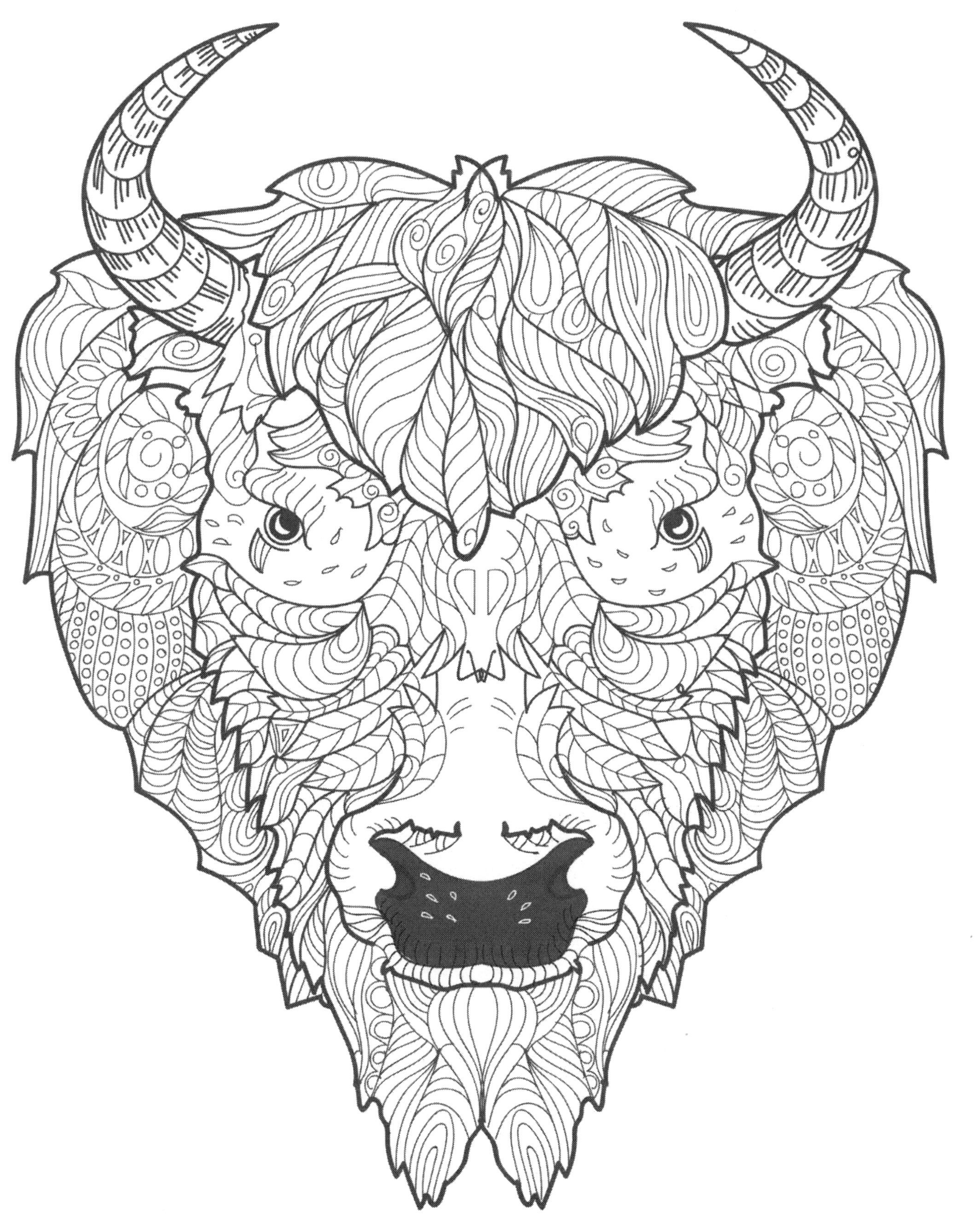

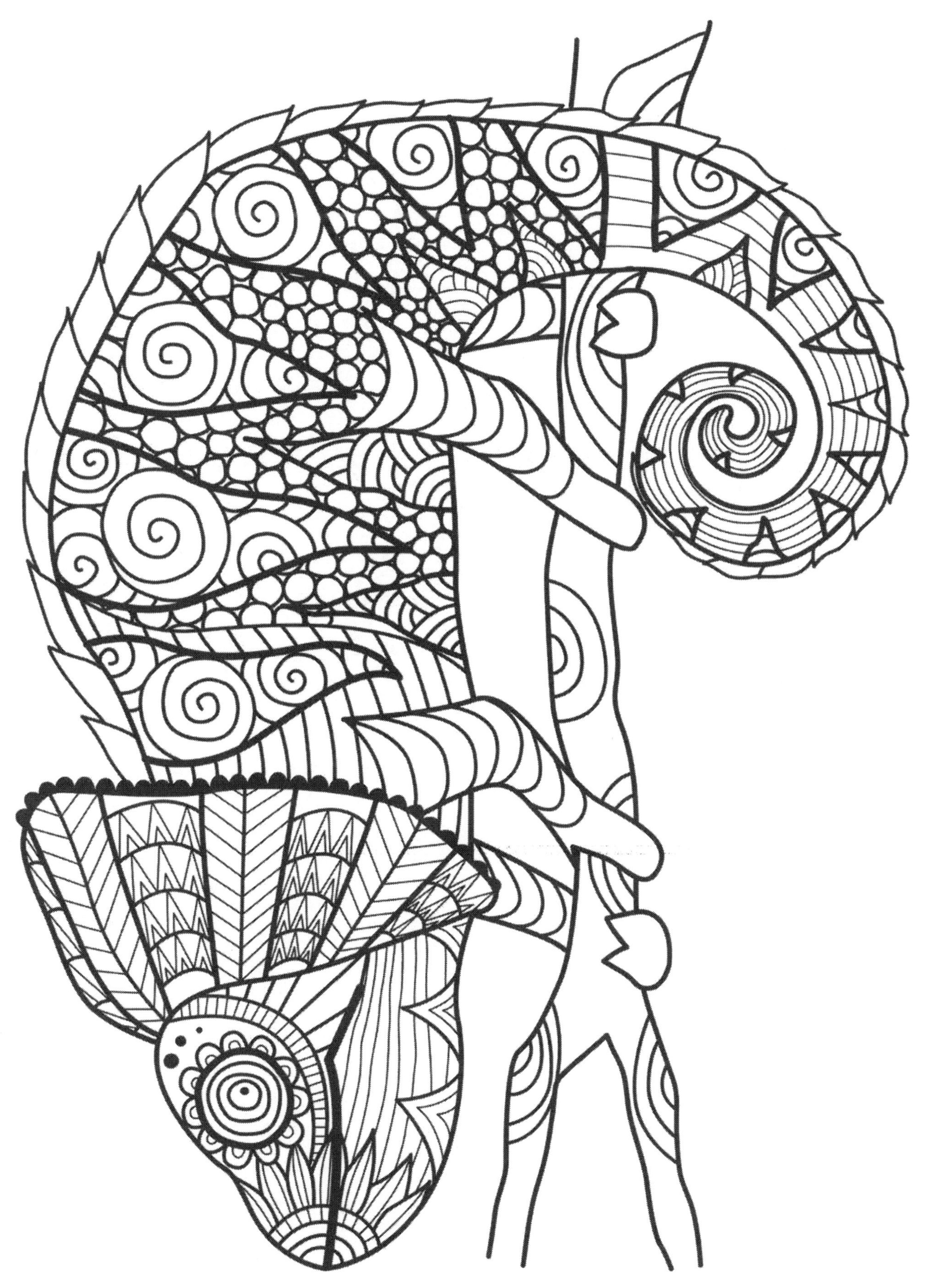

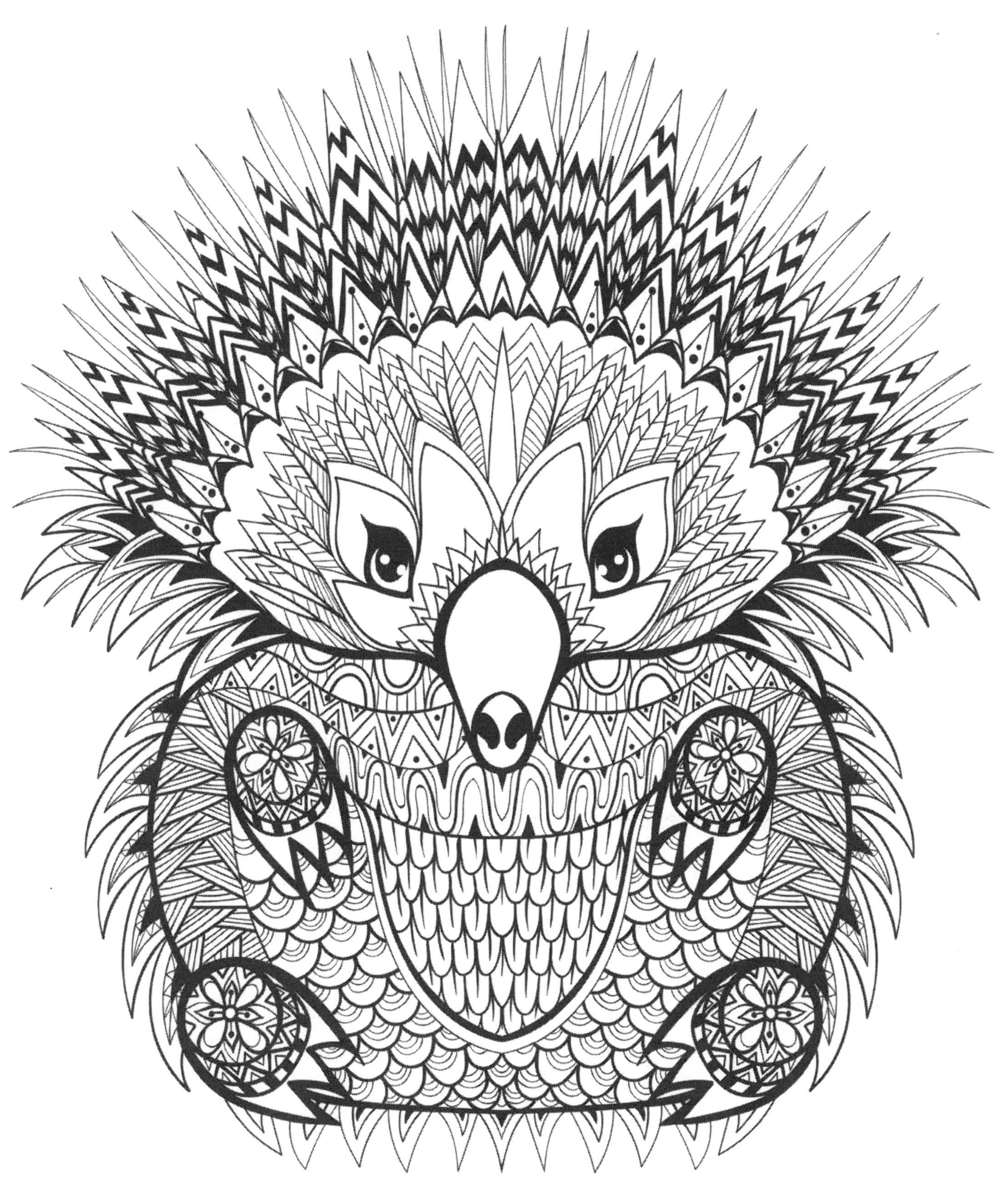

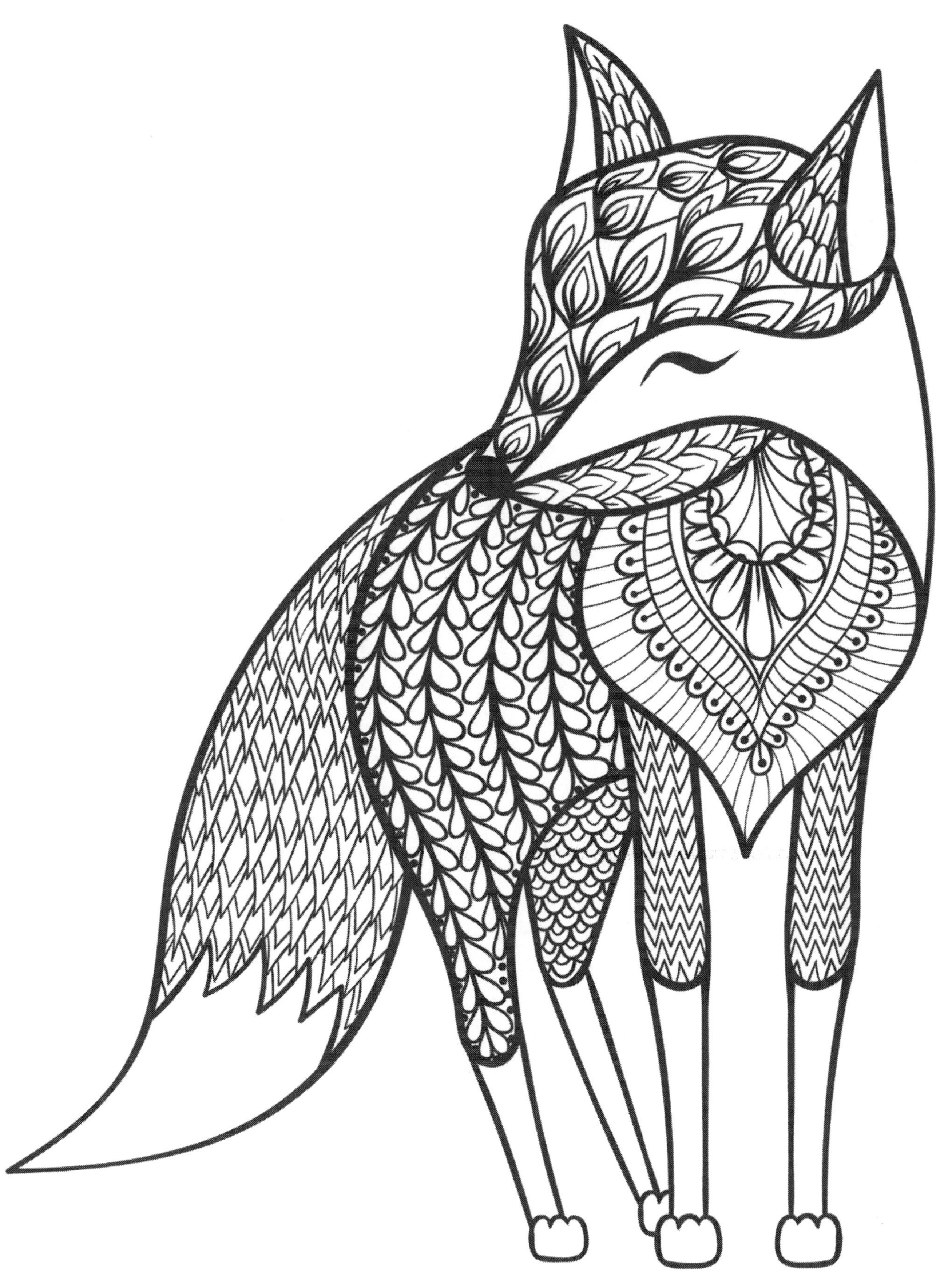

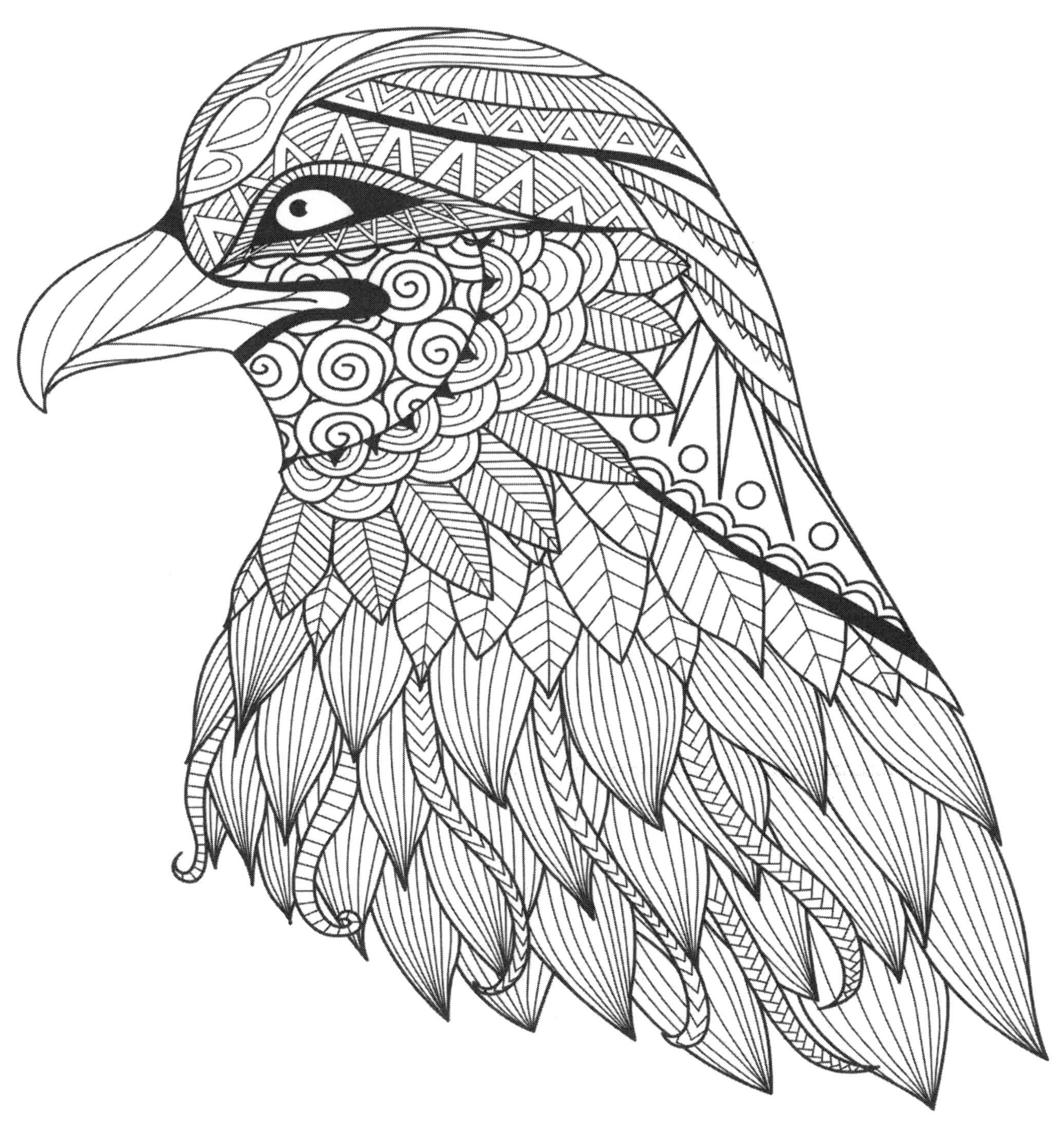

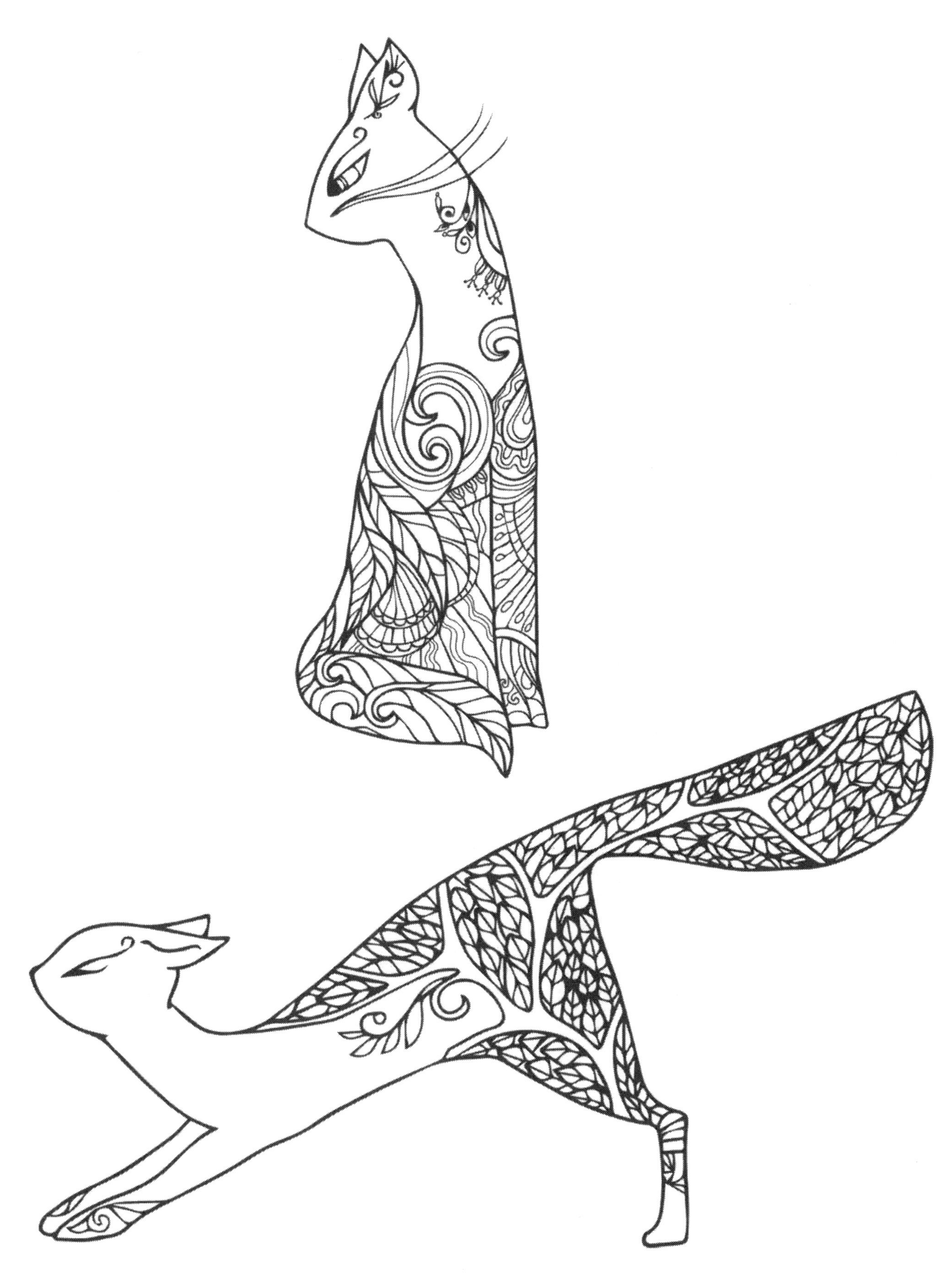

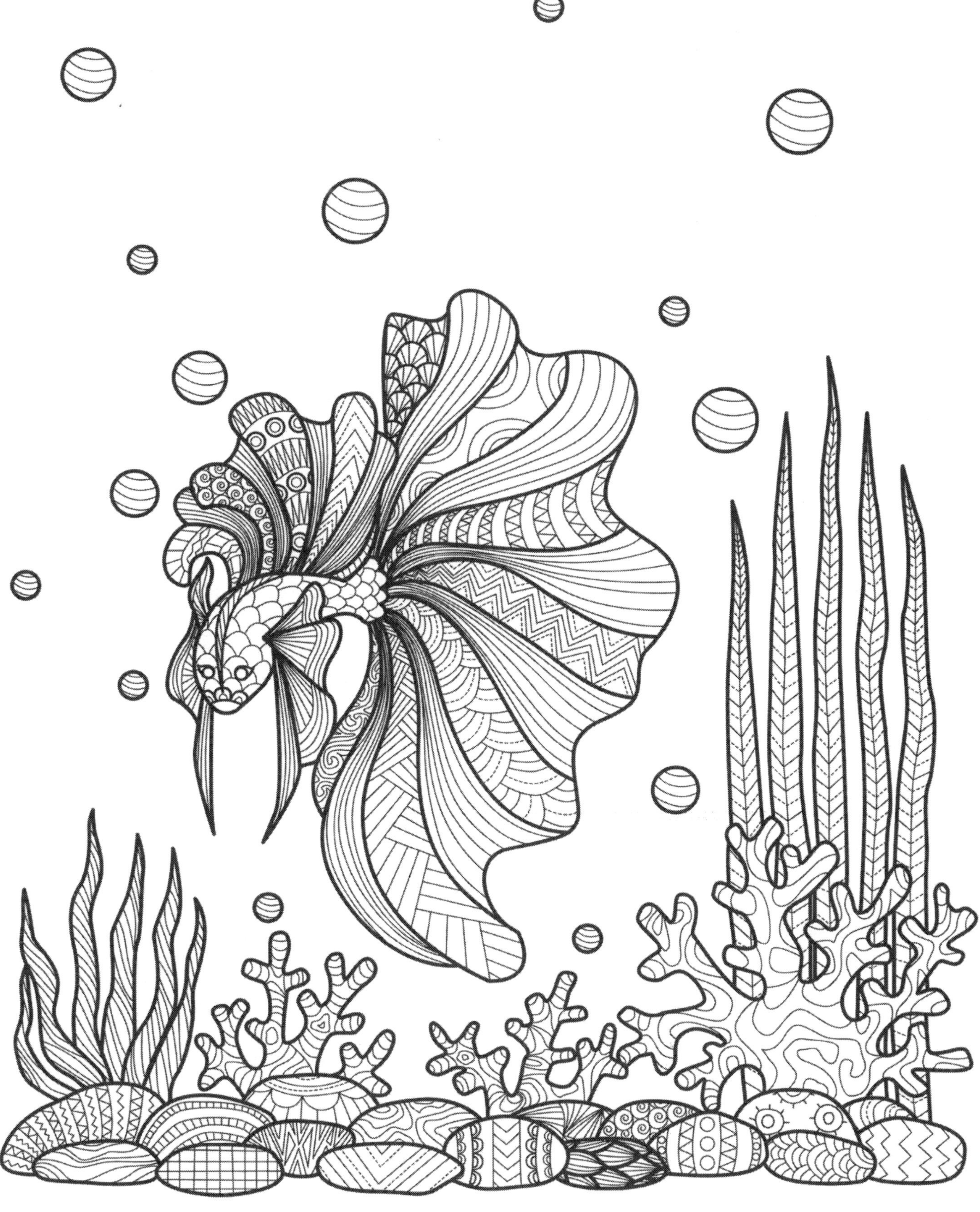

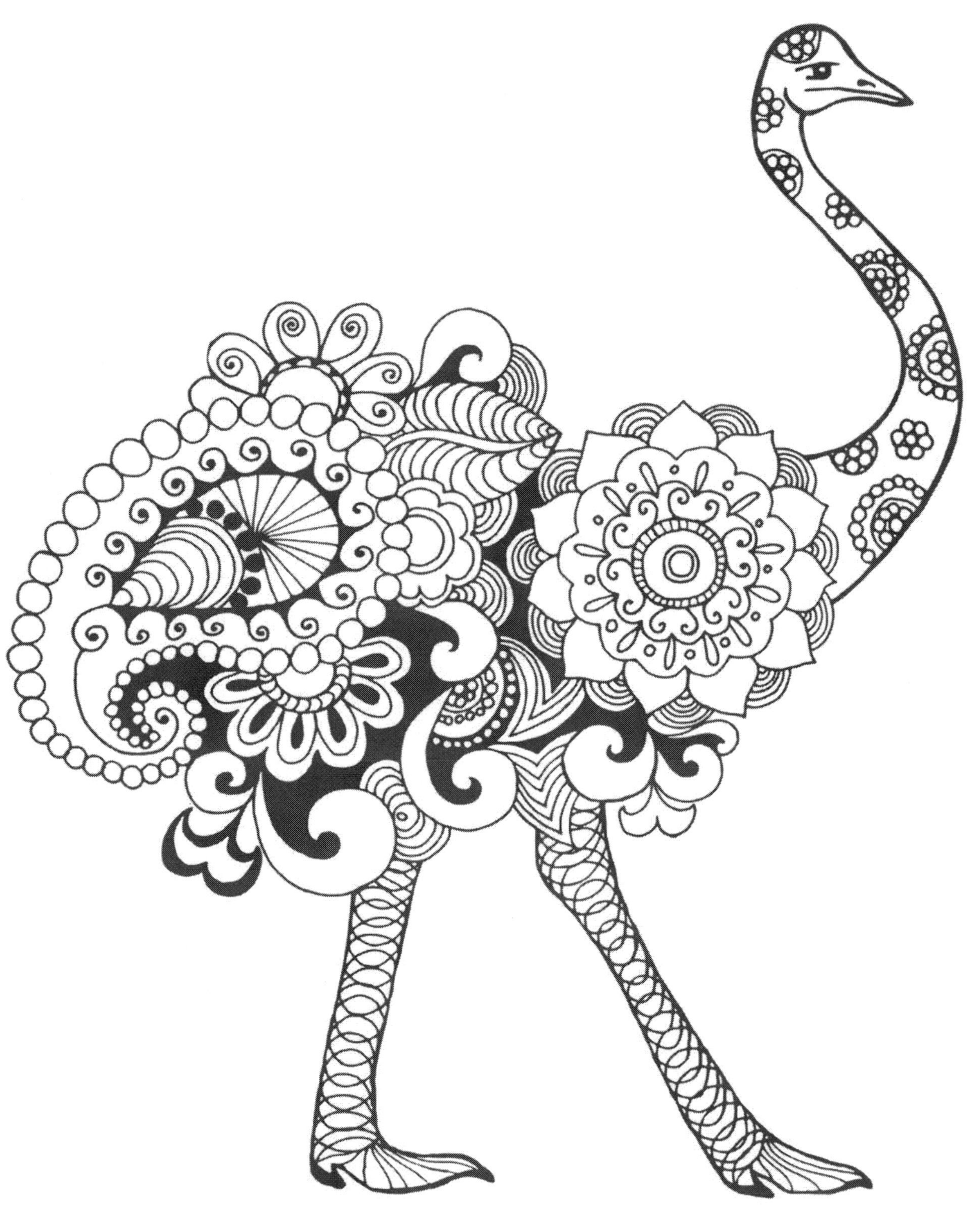

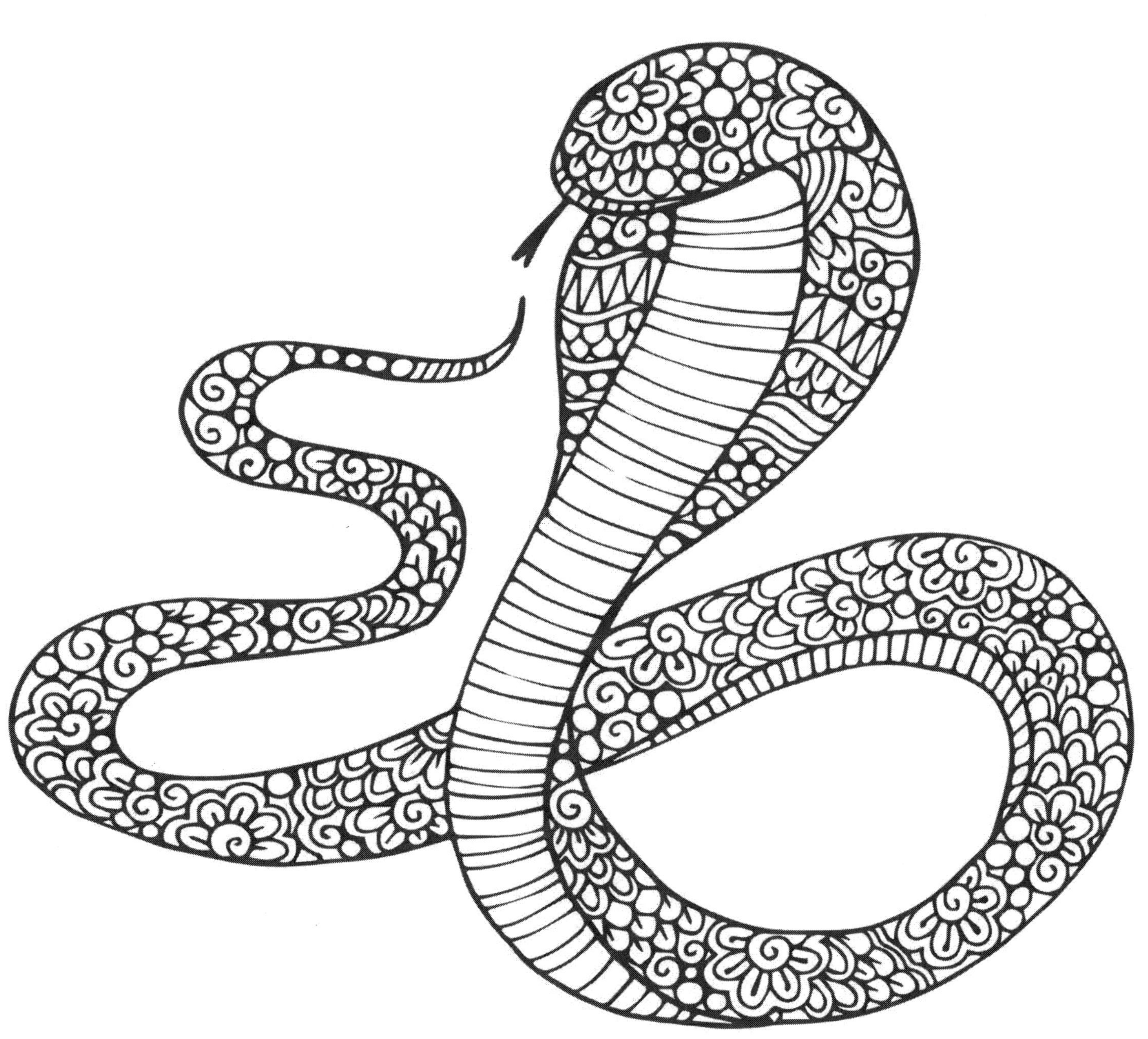

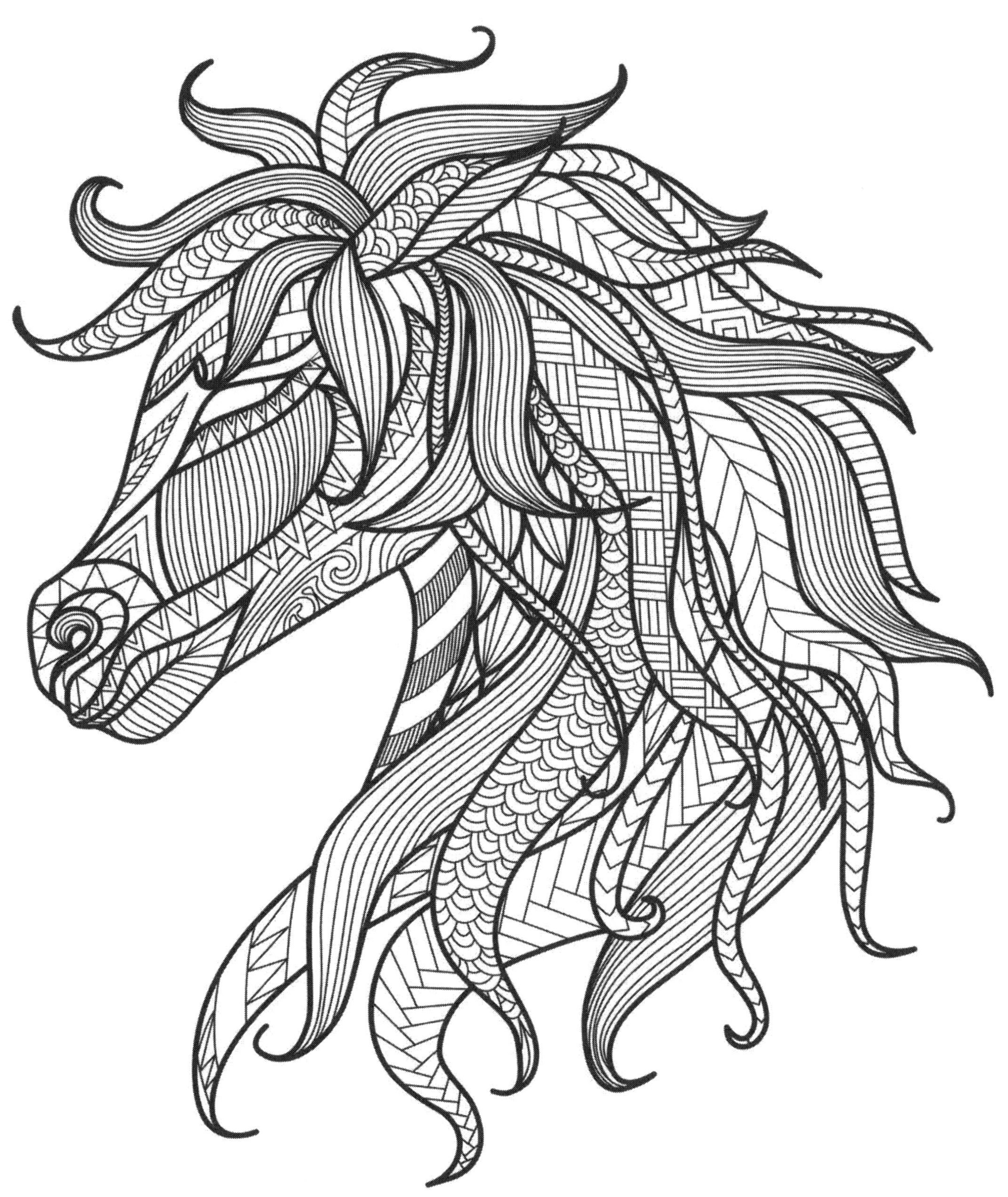

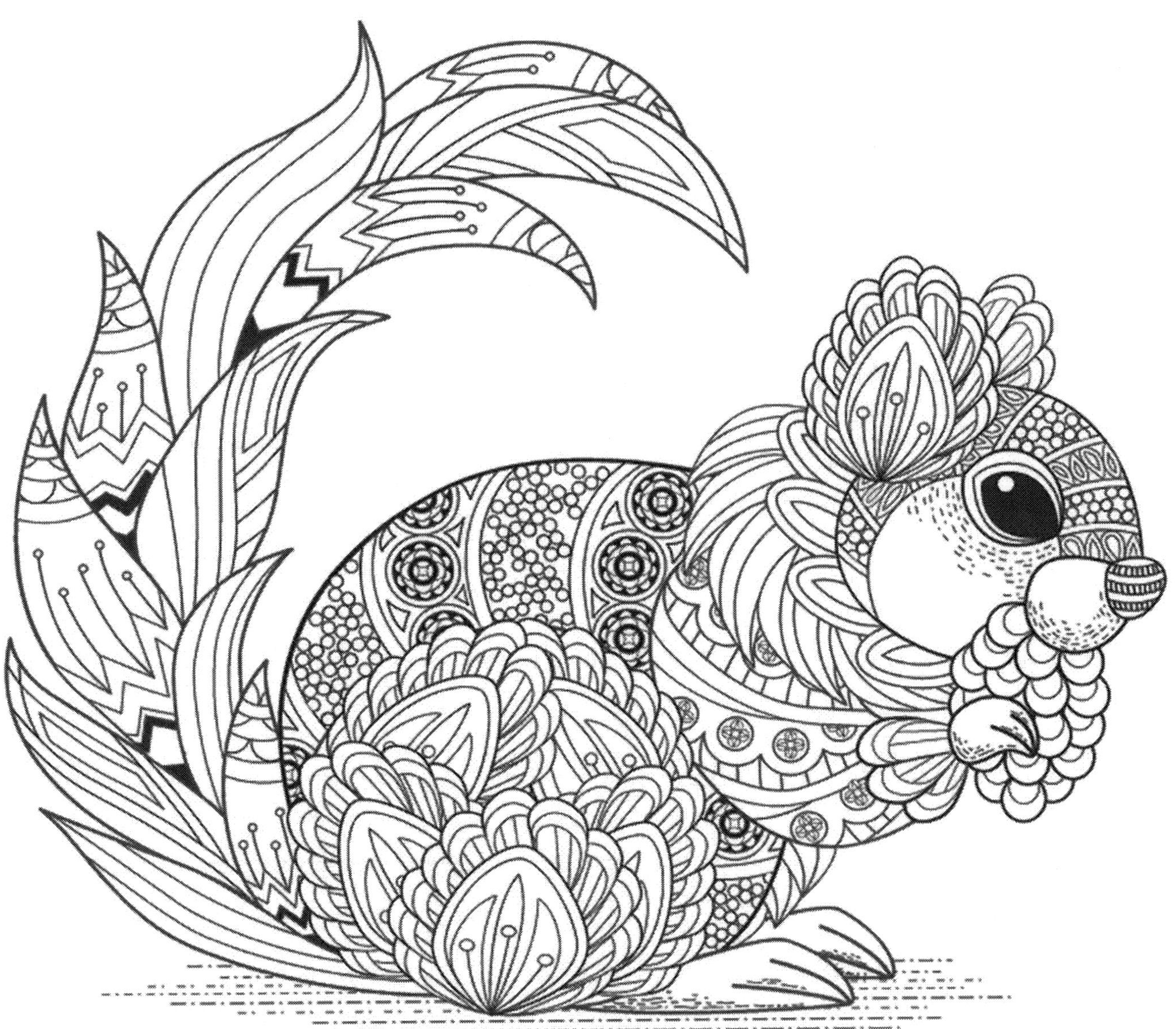

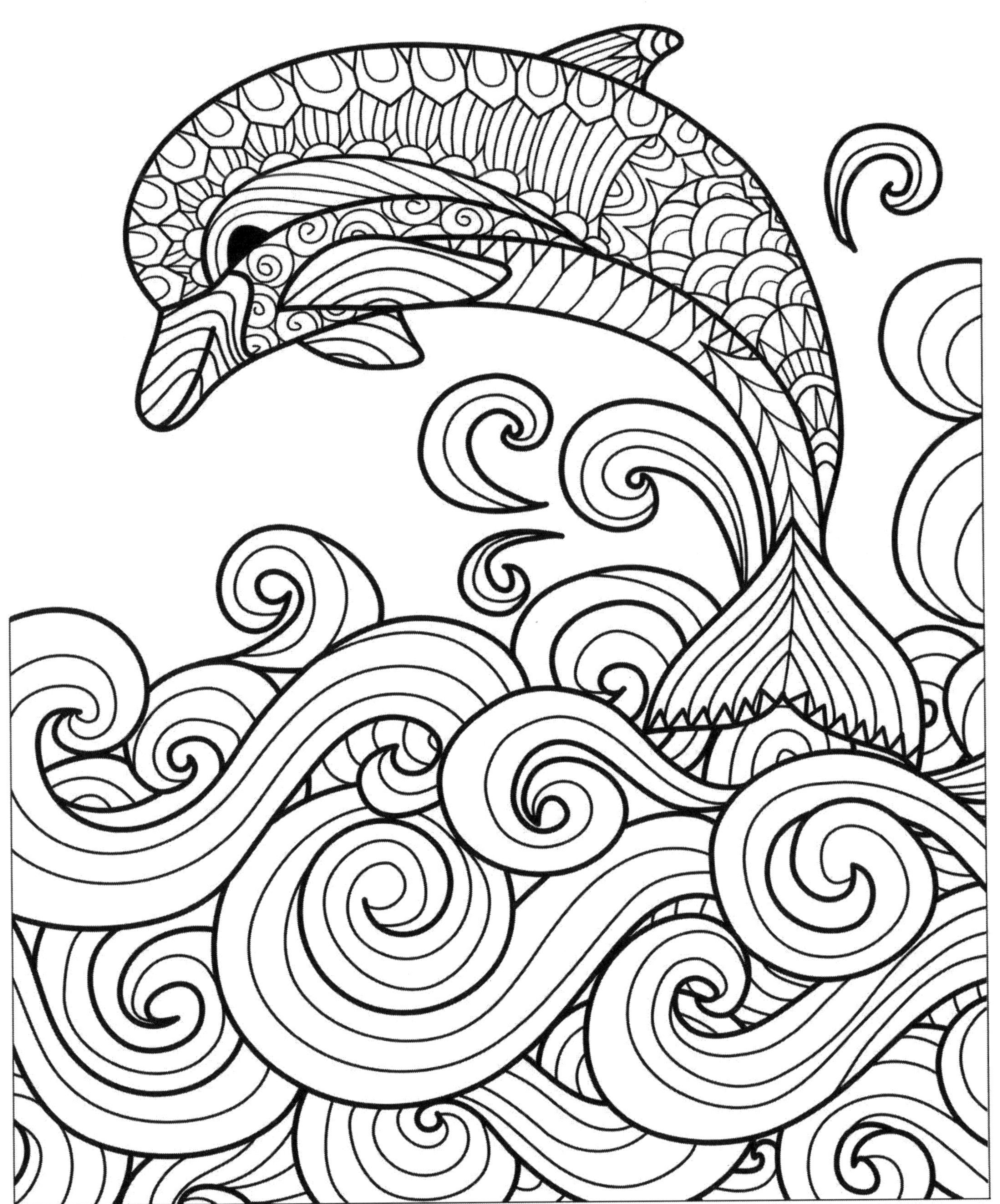

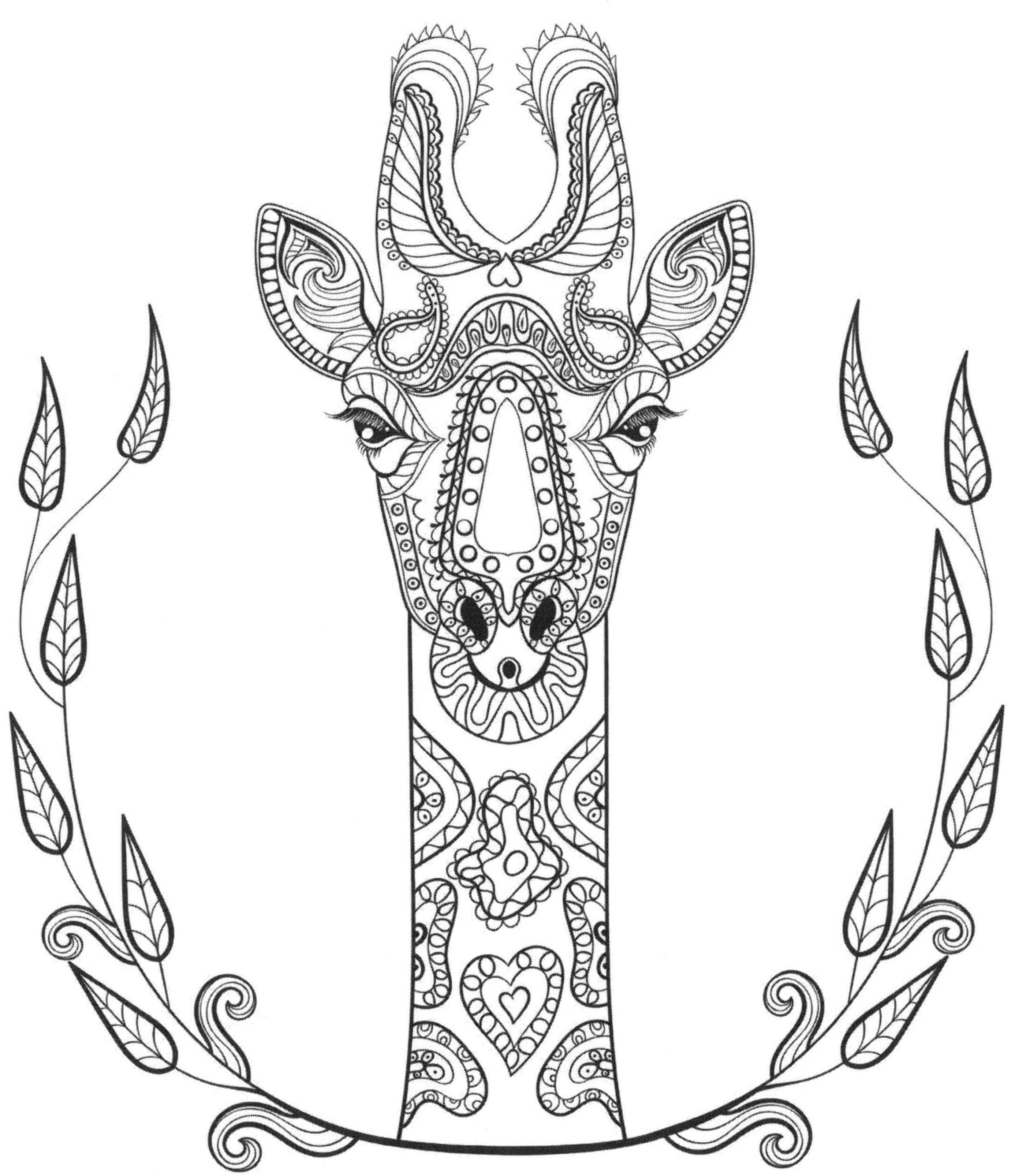

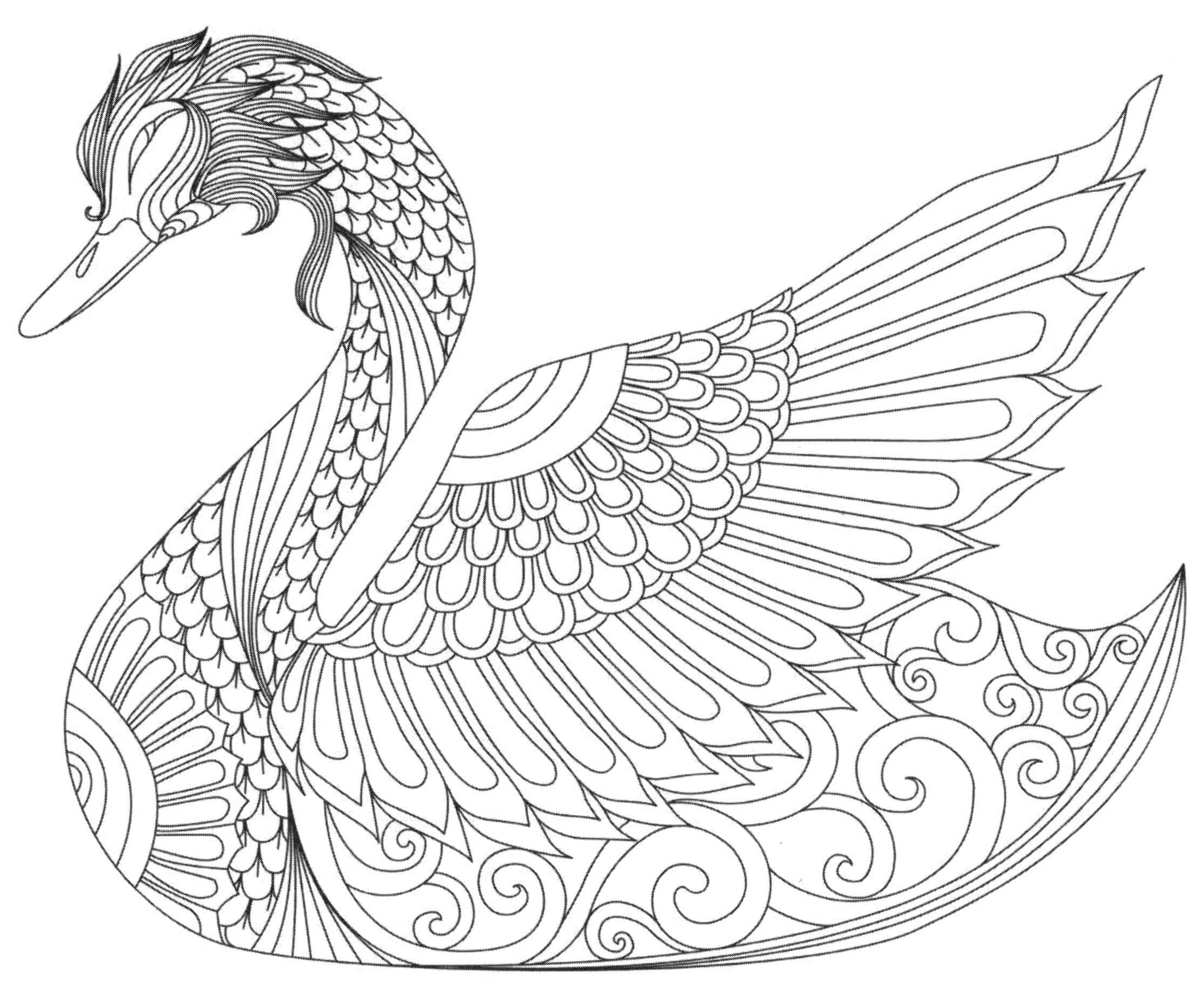

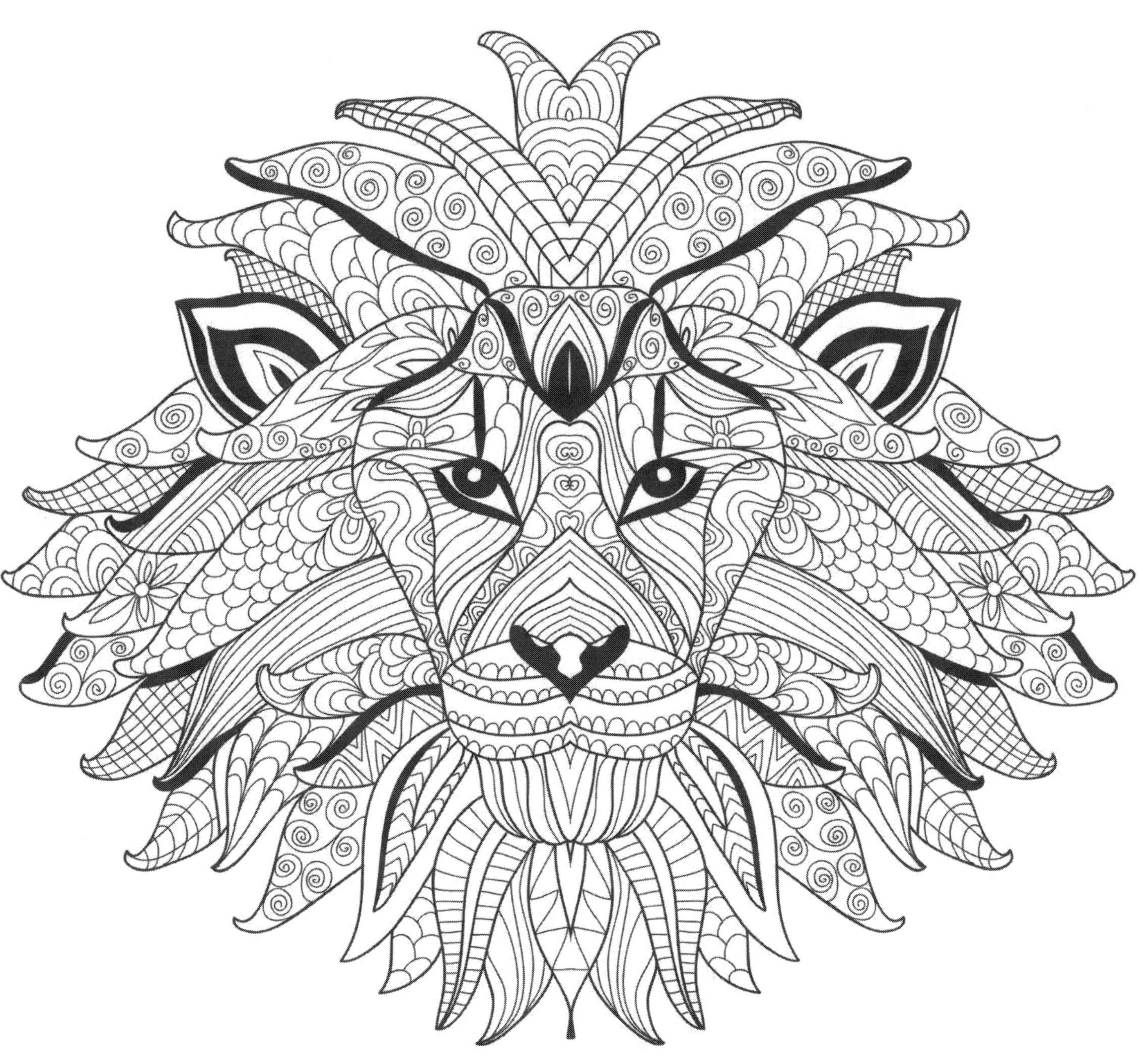

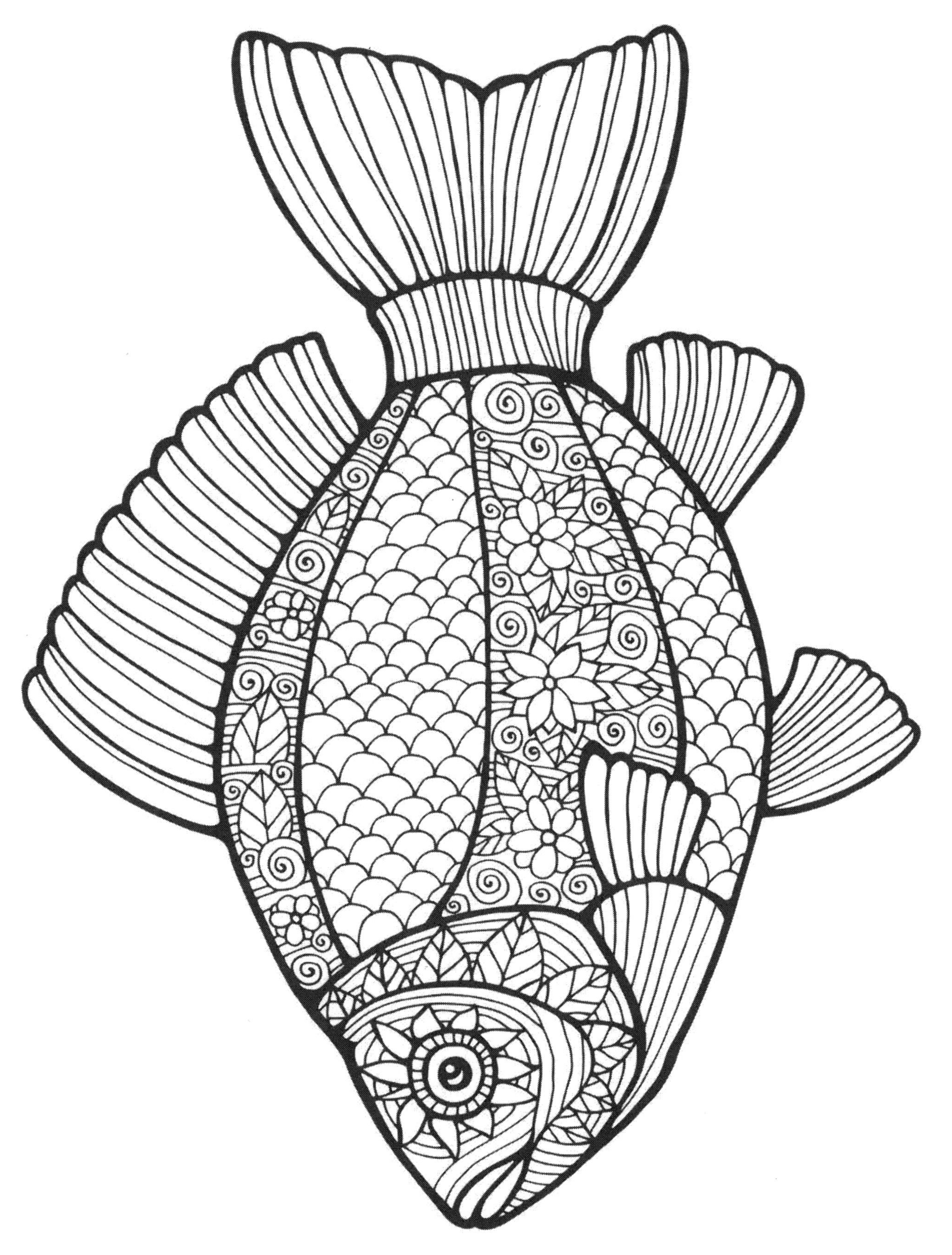

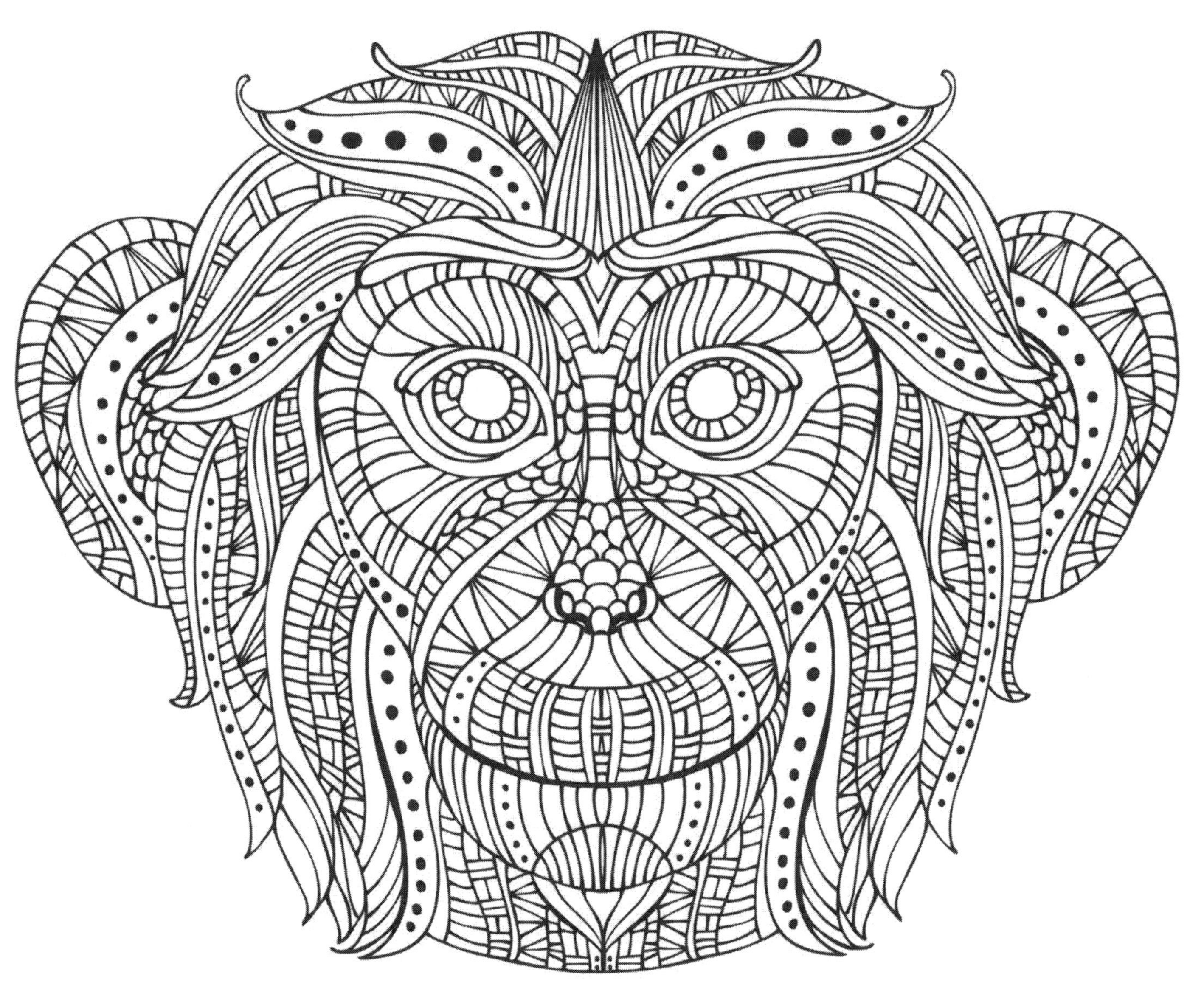

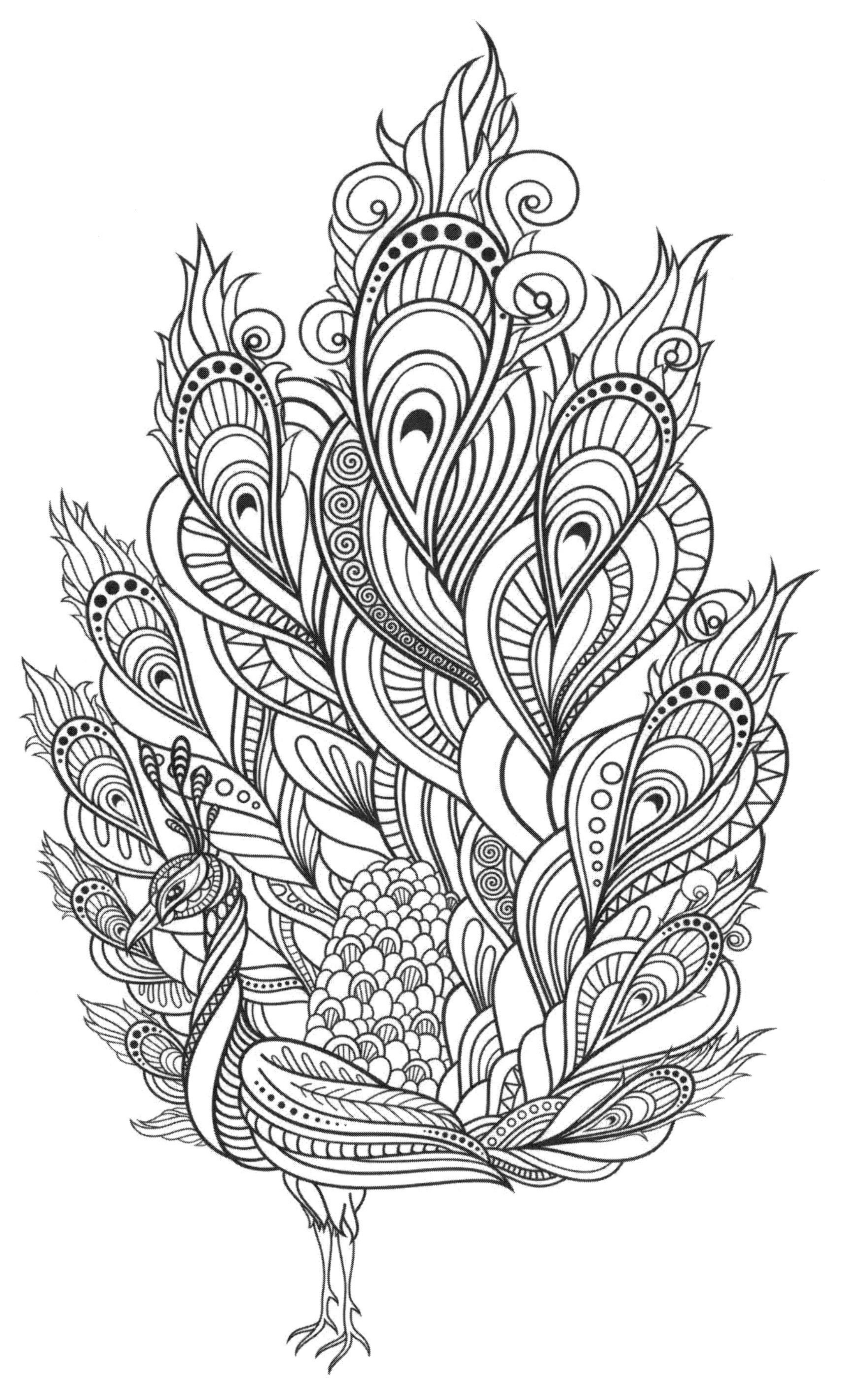

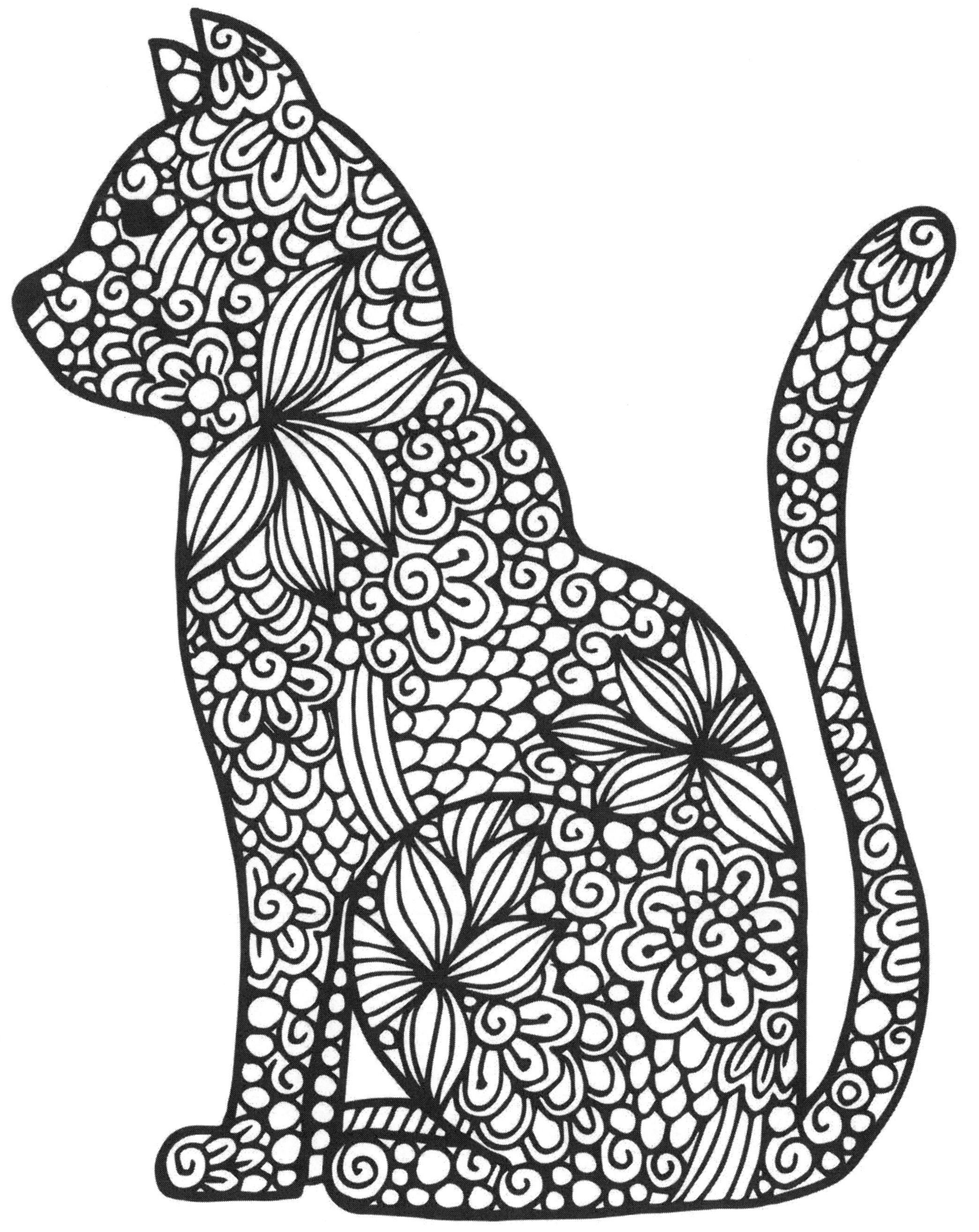

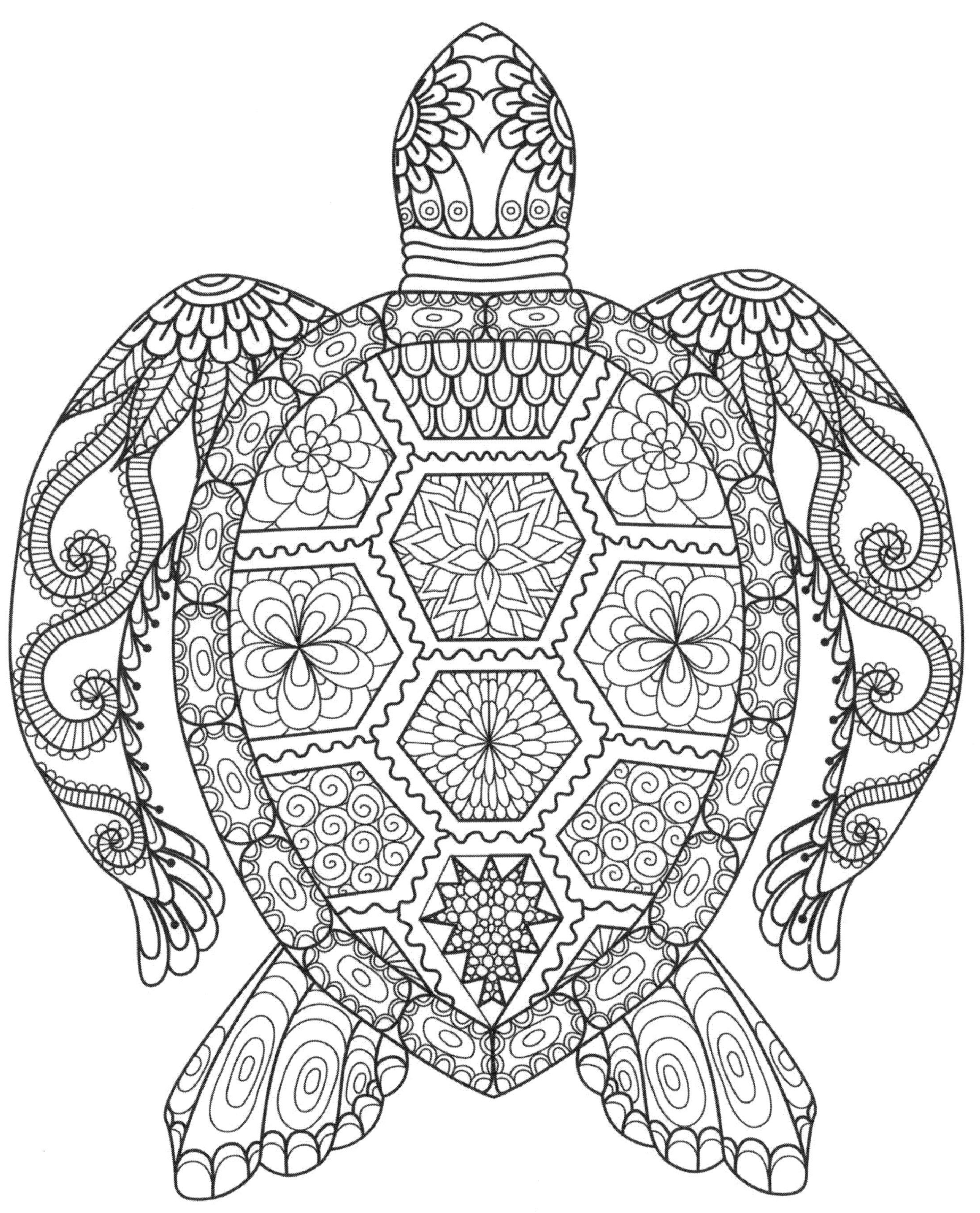

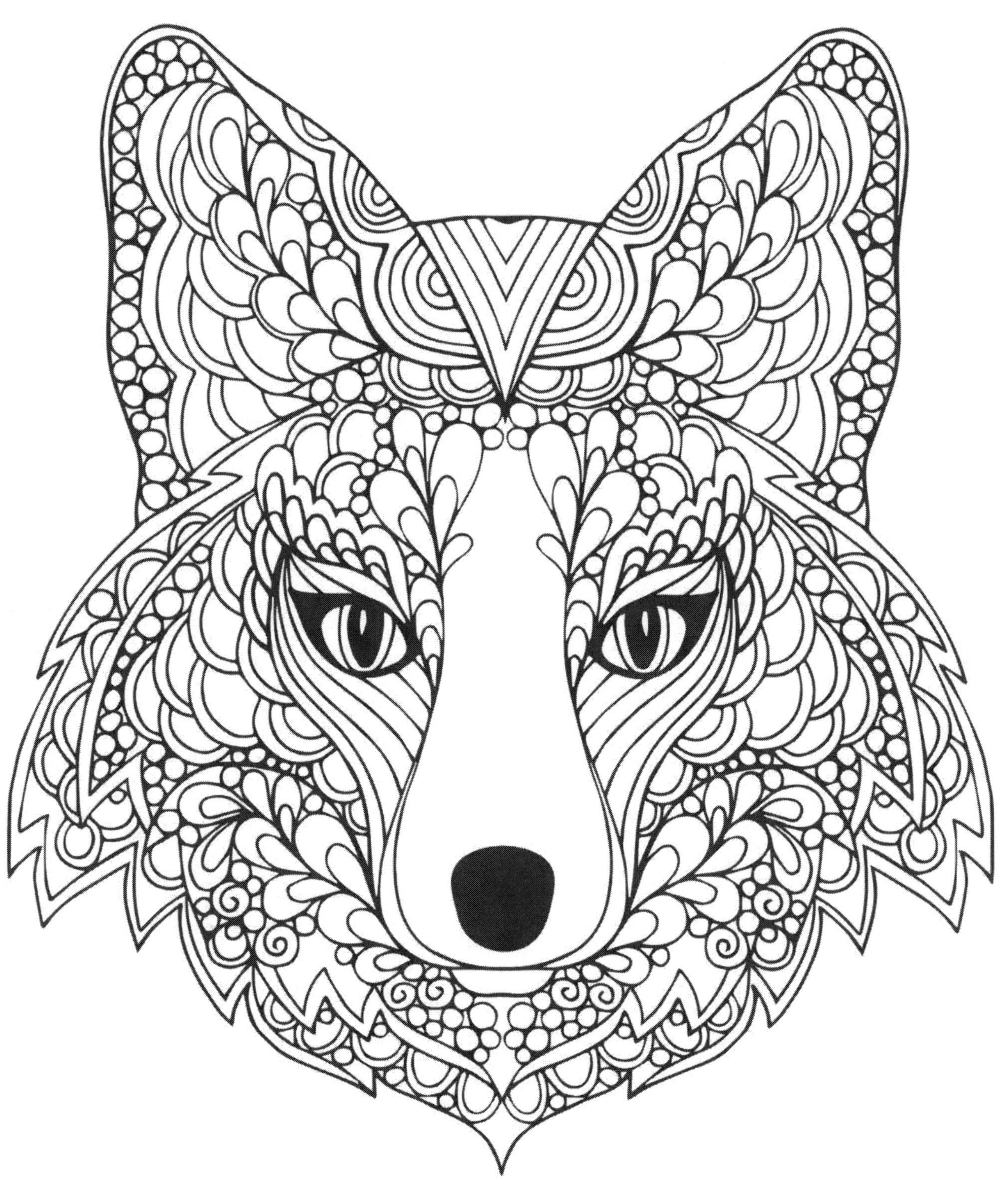

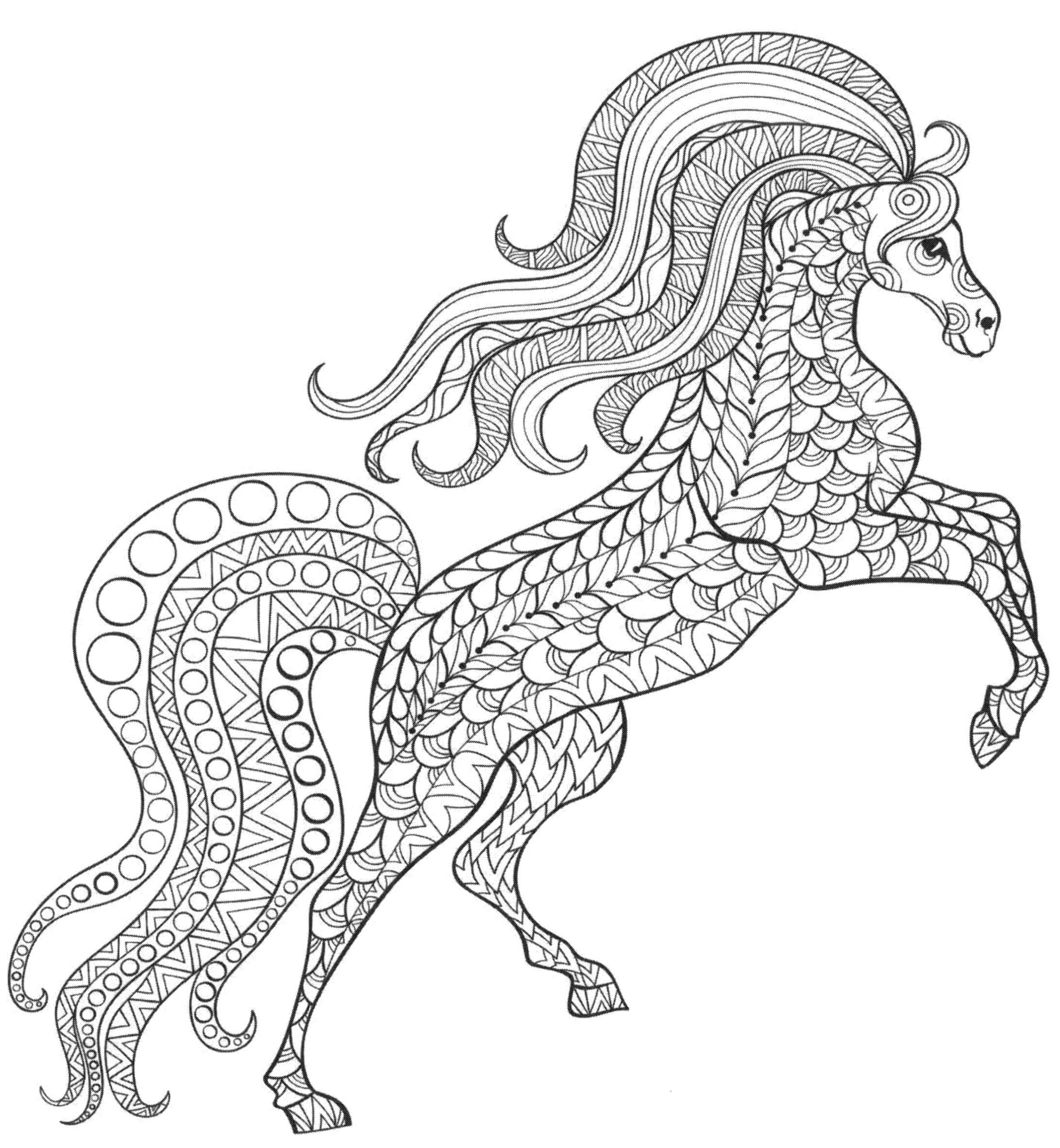

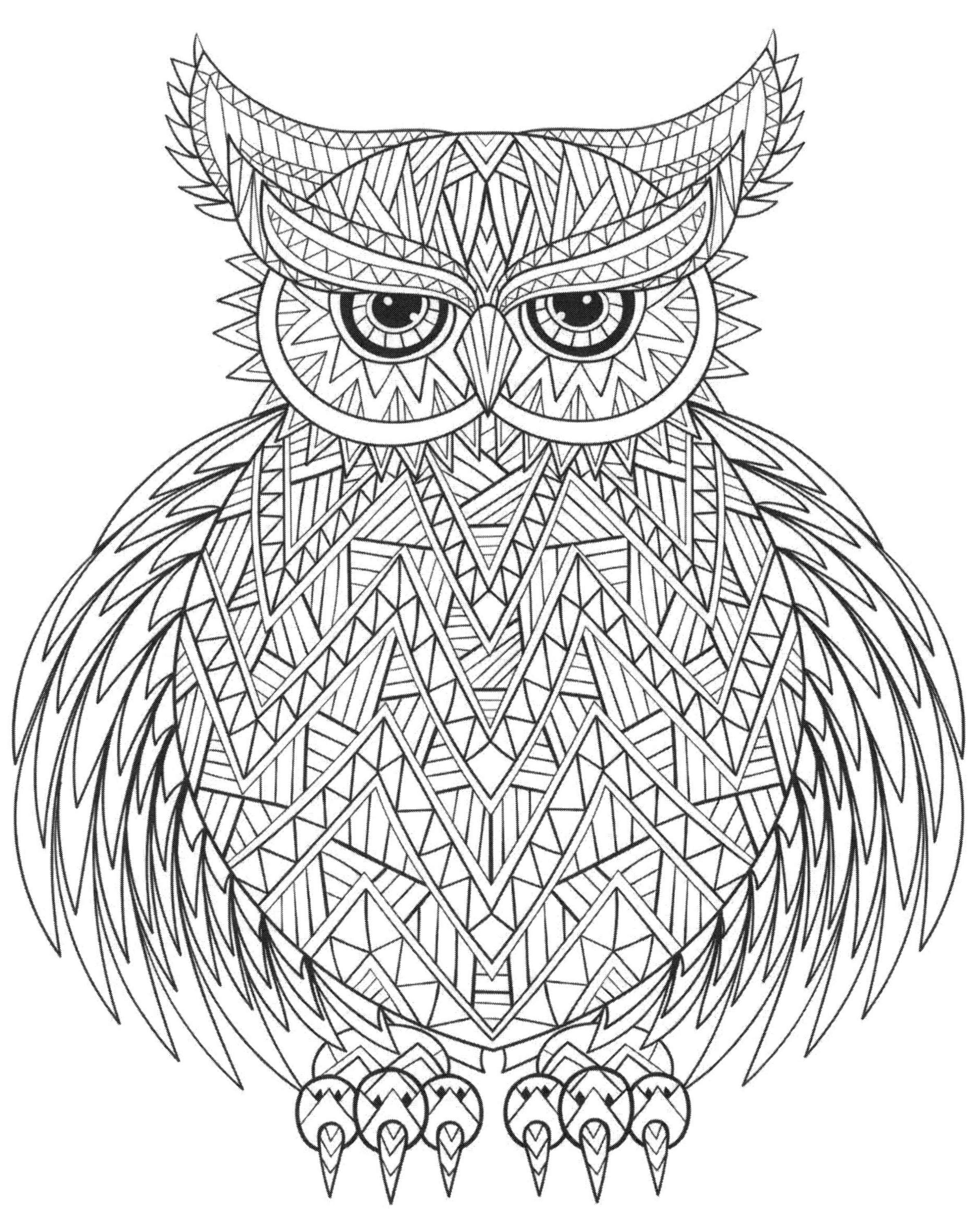

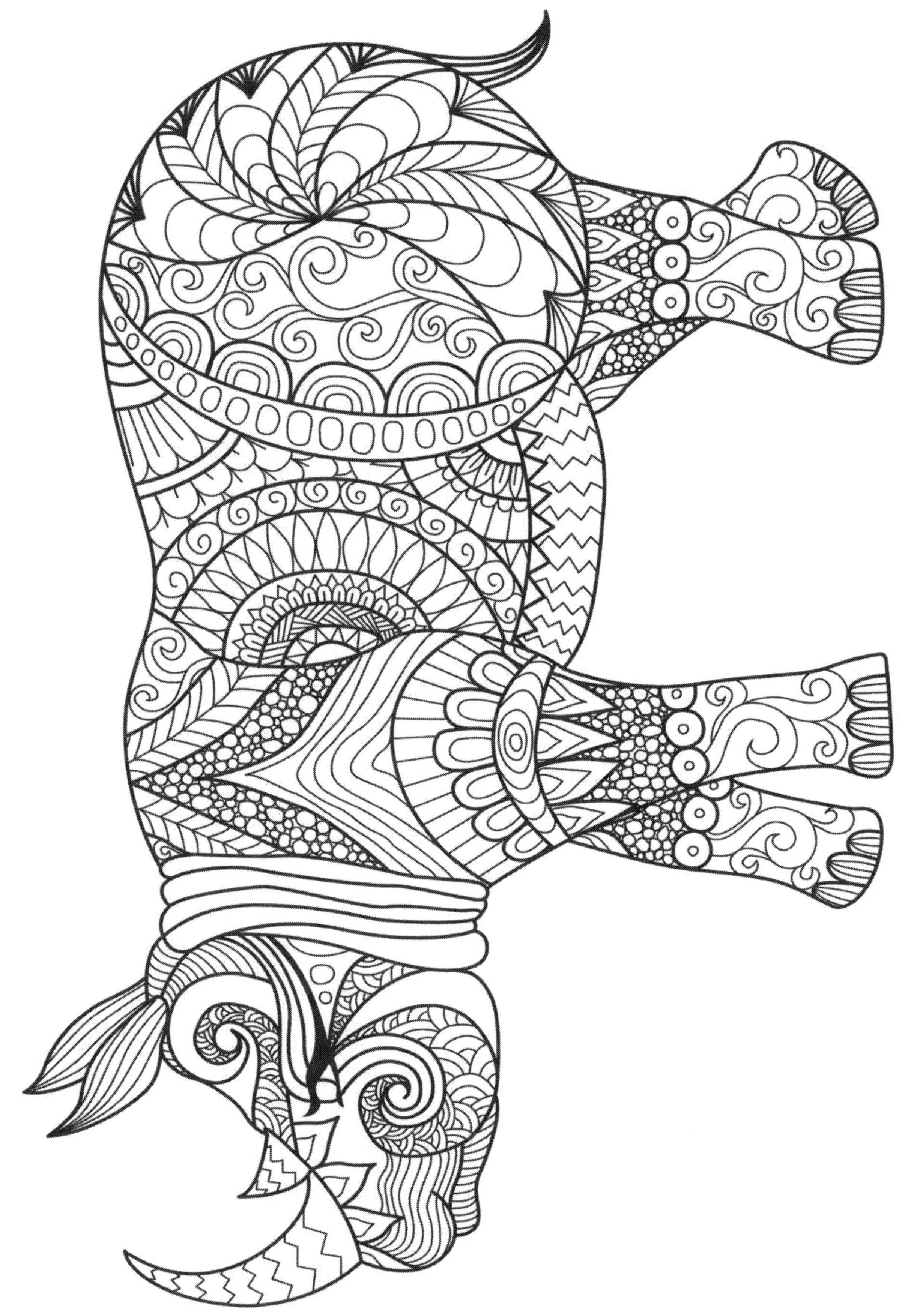

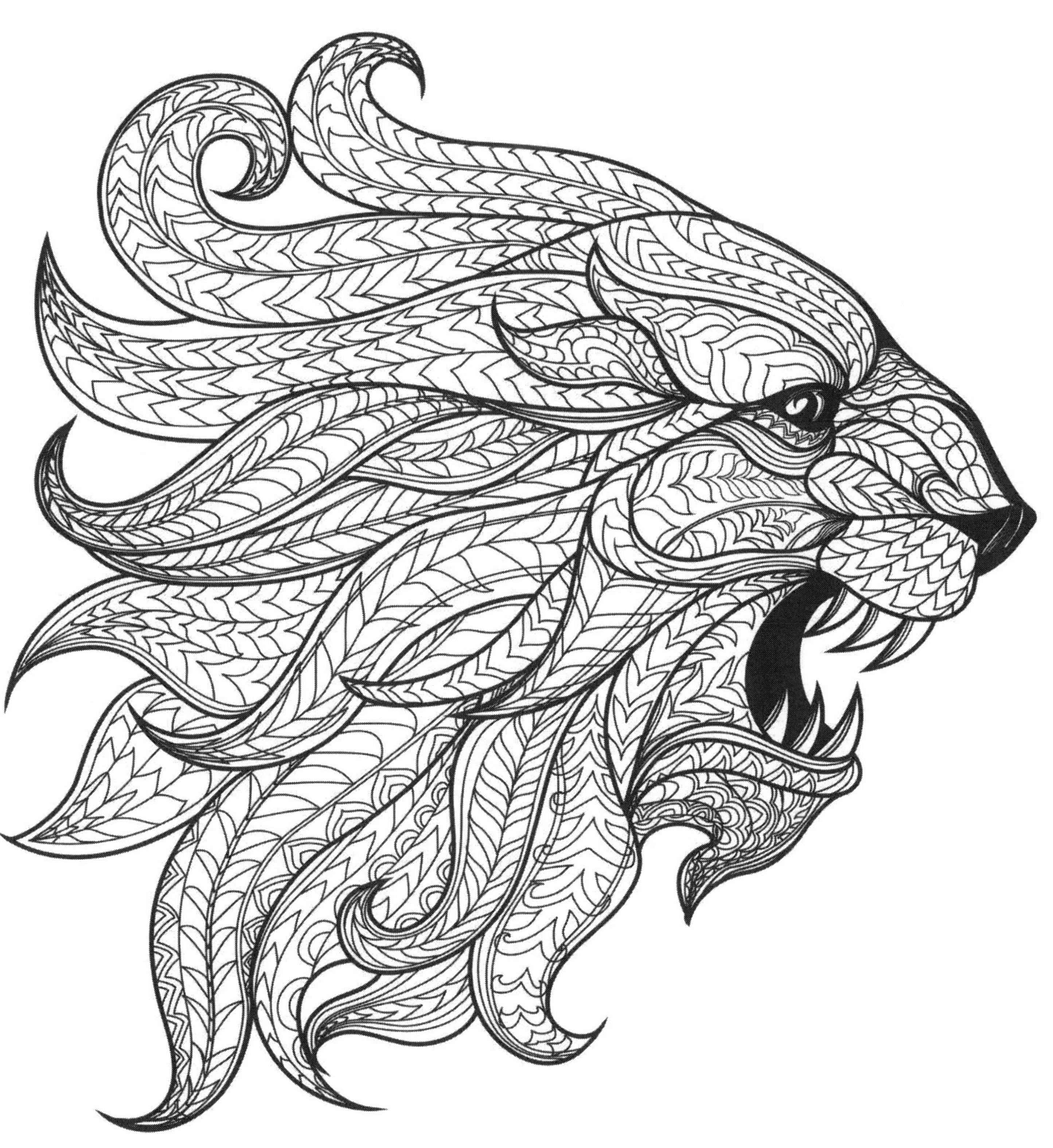

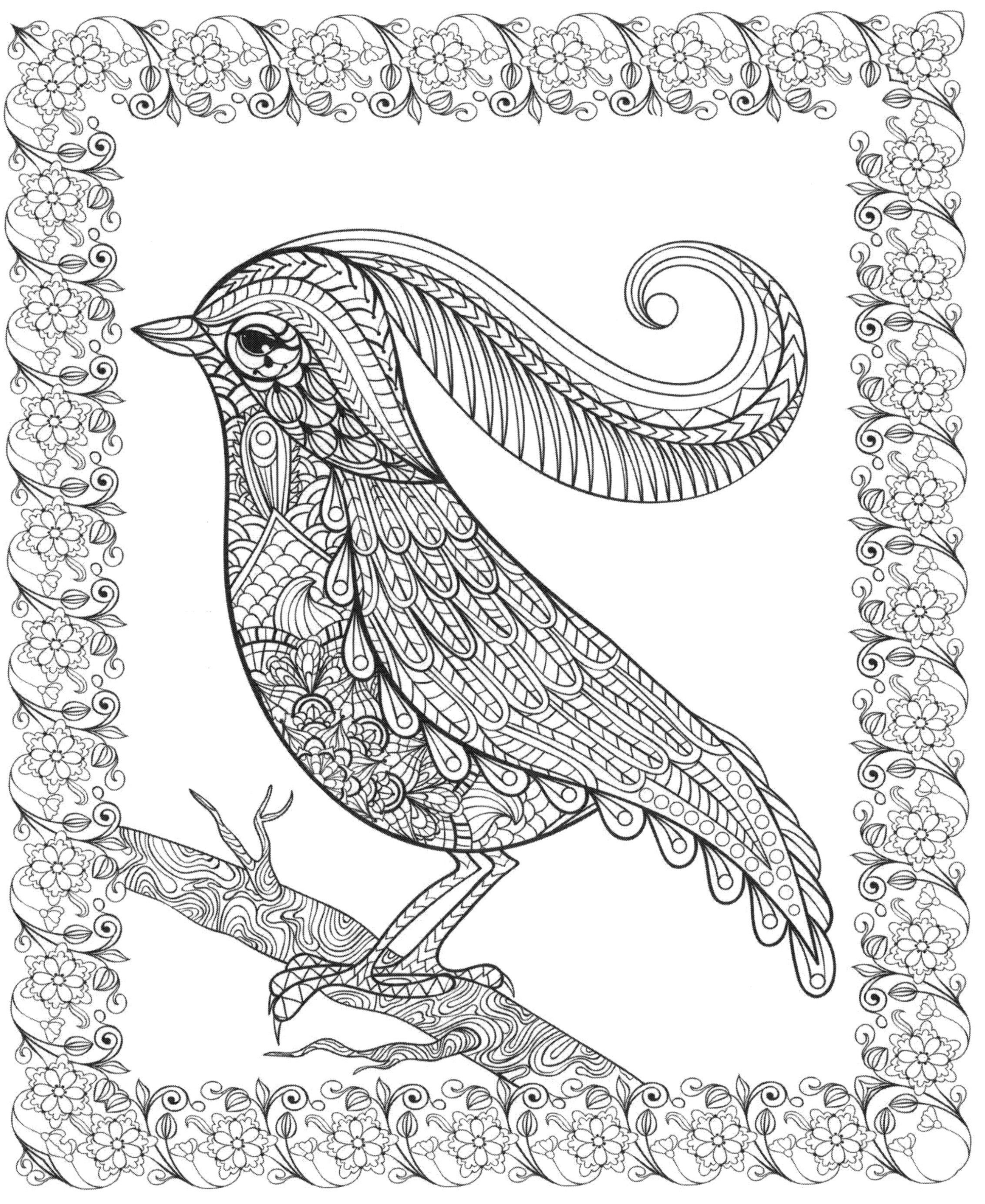

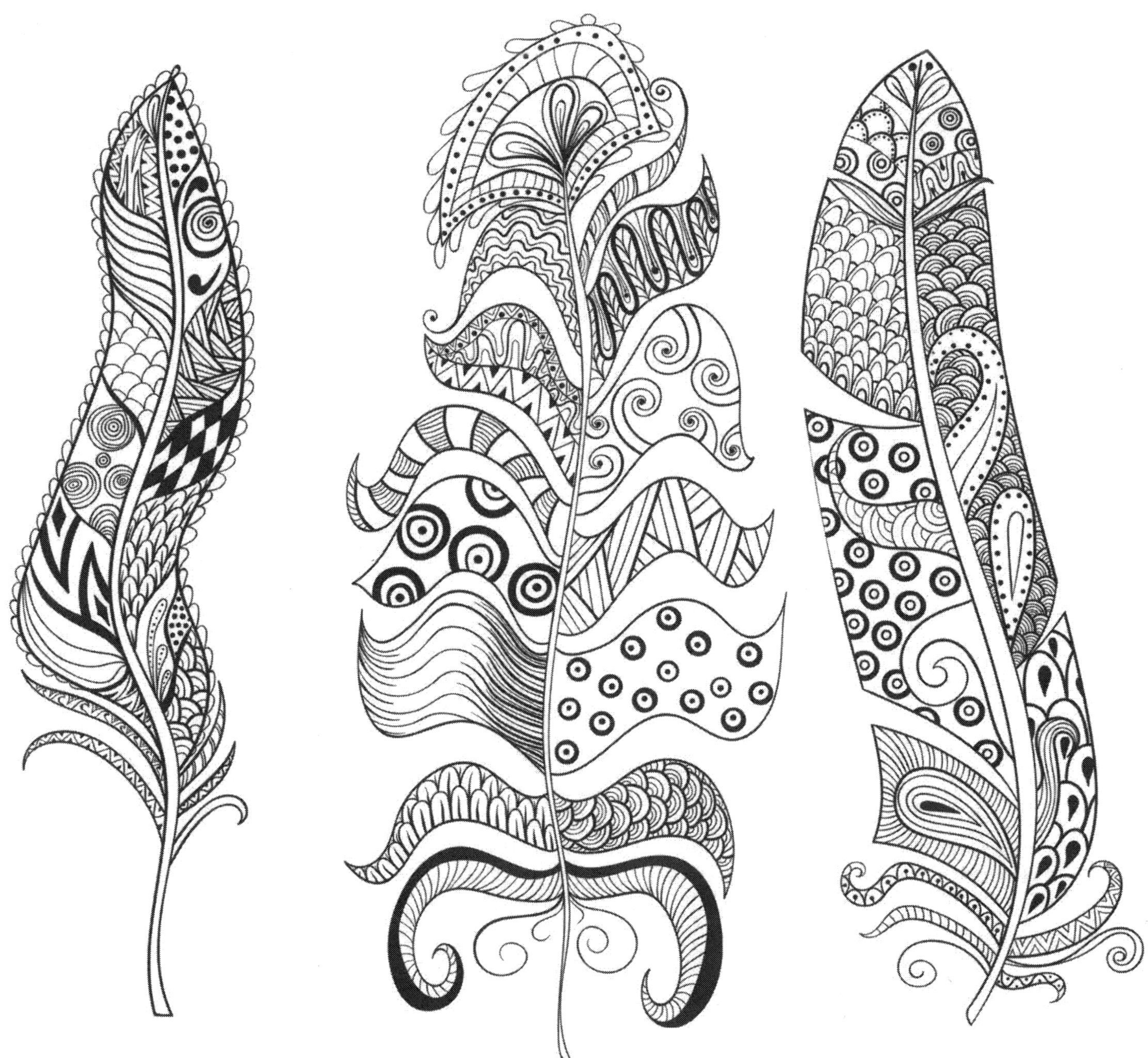

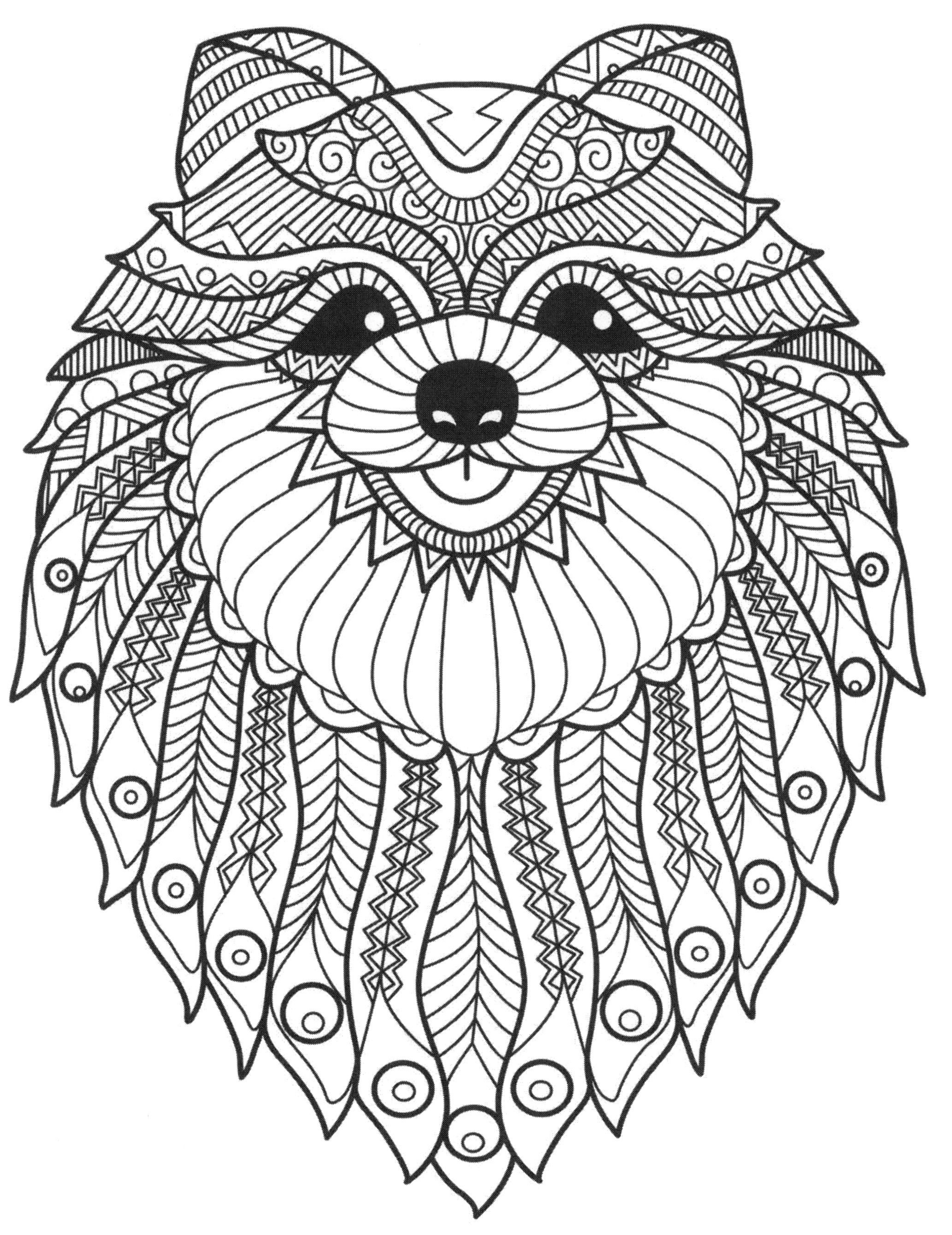

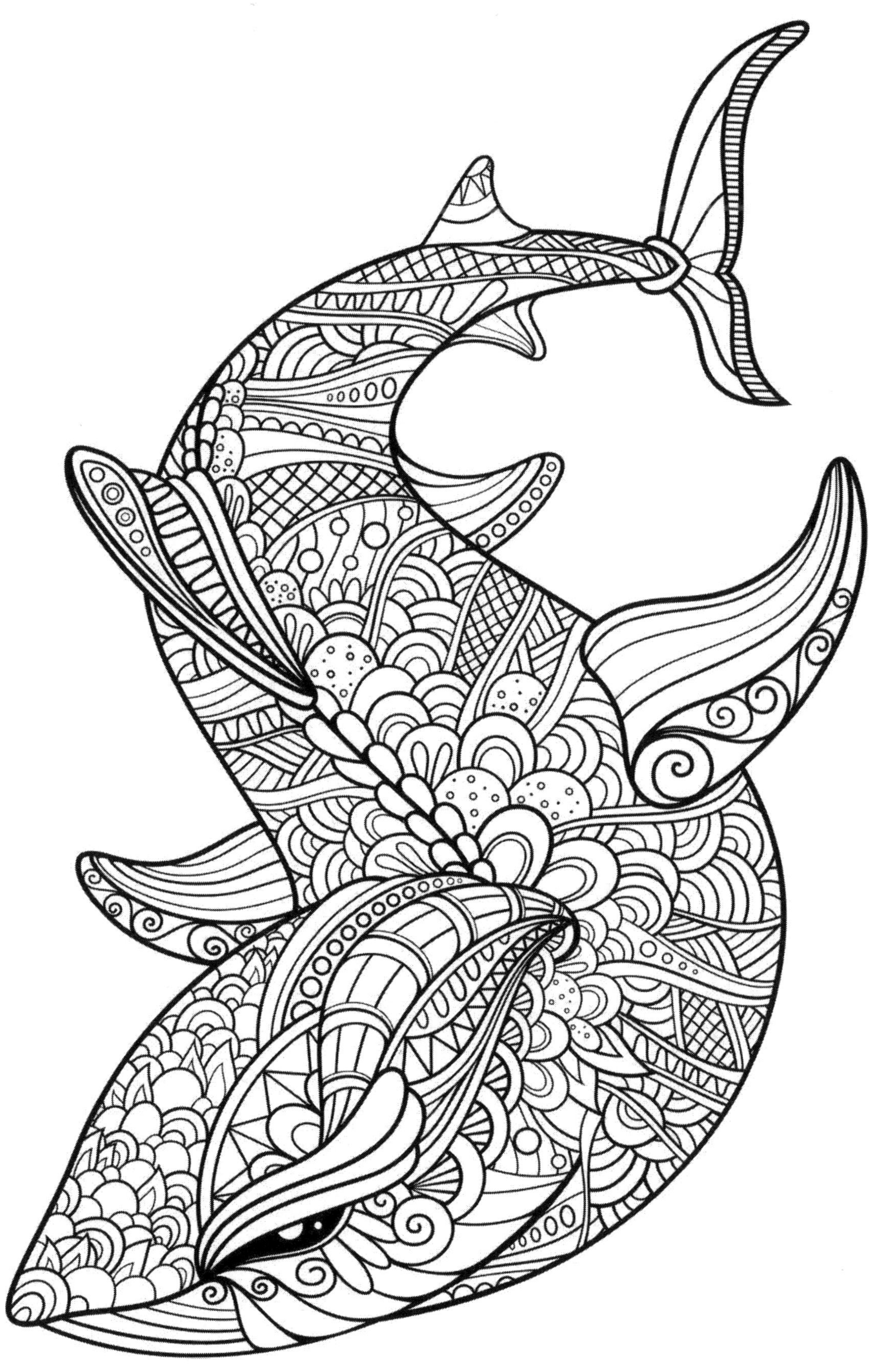

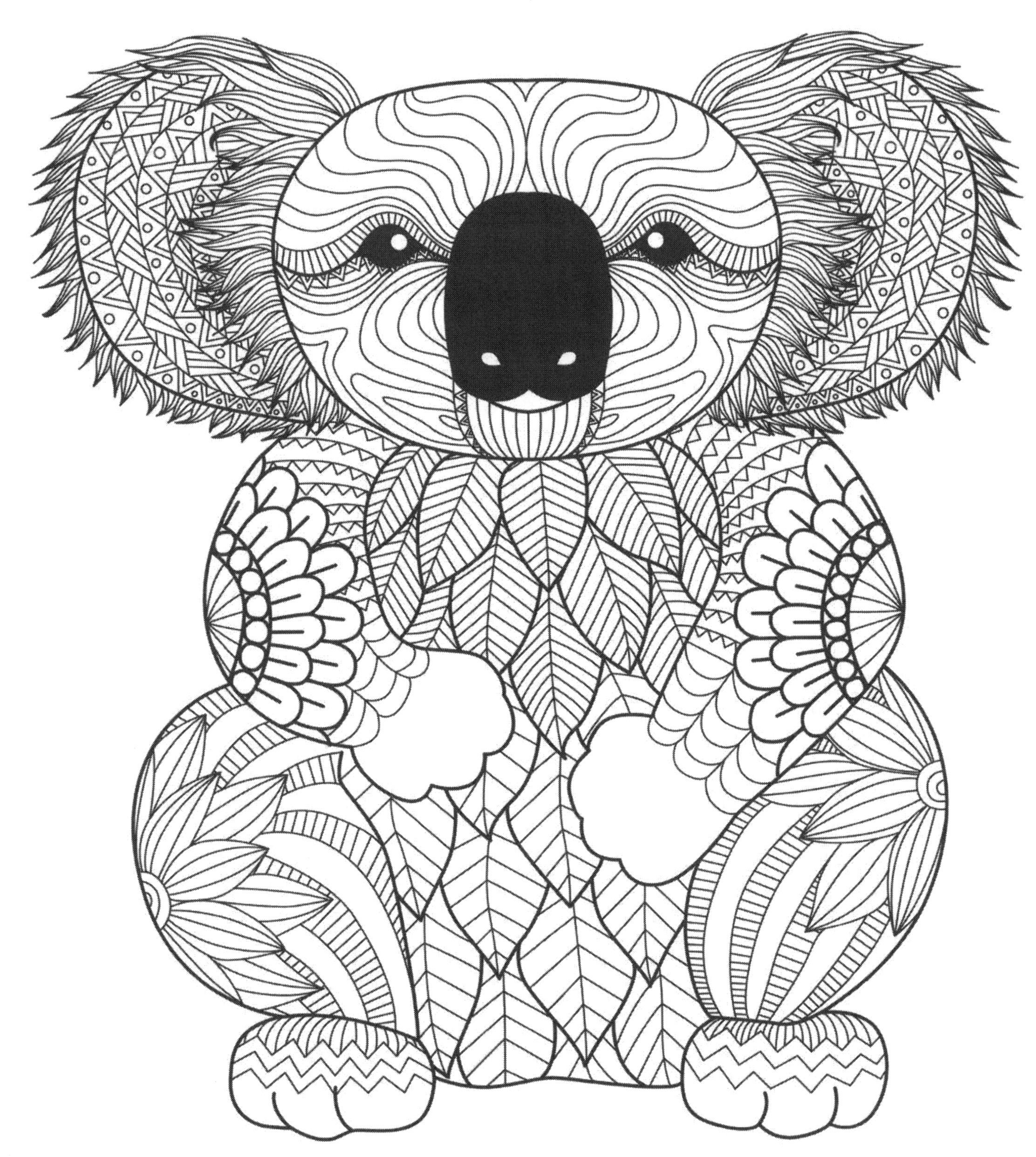

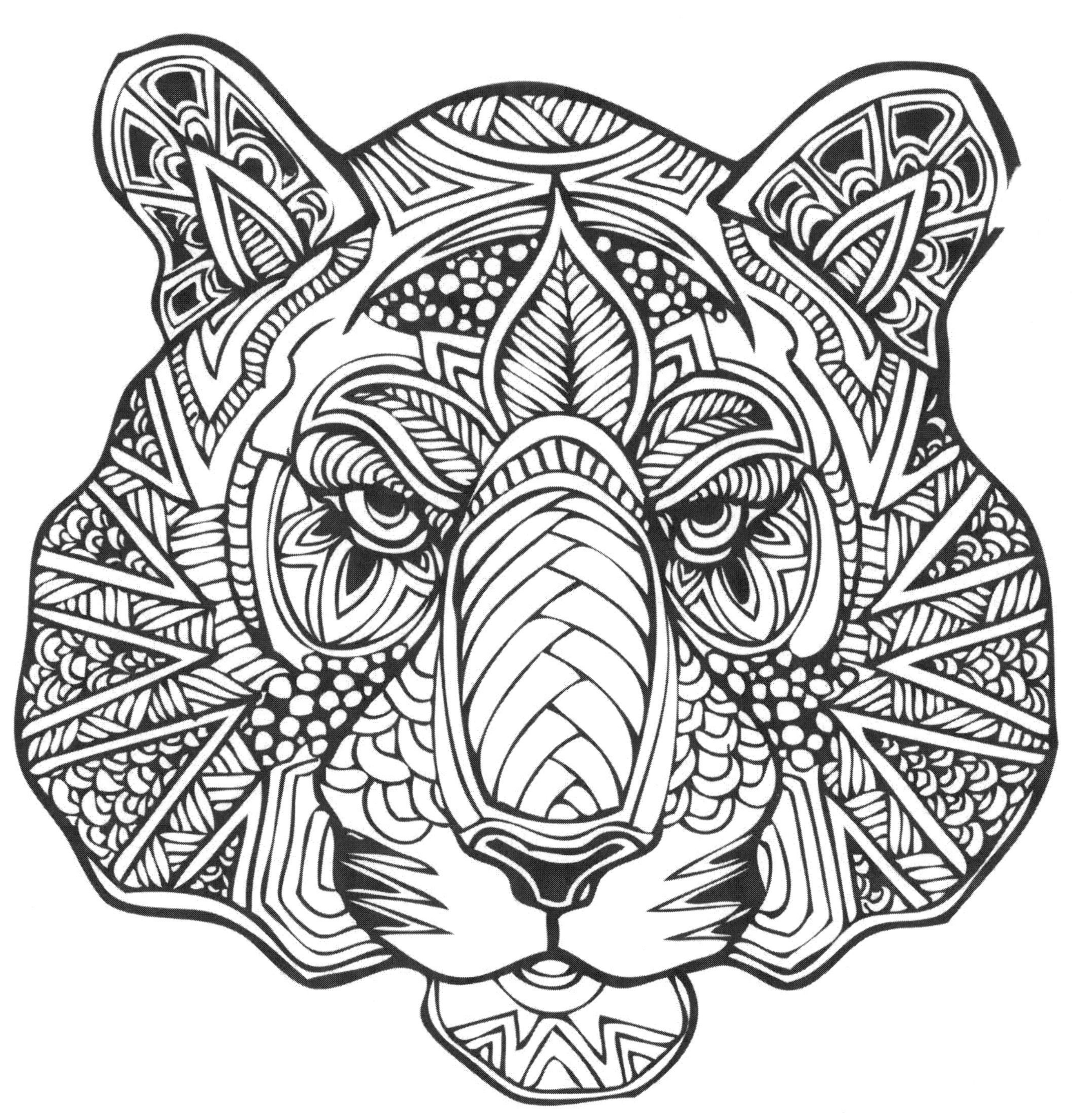

Made in the USA
Lexington, KY
17 December 2016